MYRTLEWOOD MEMOIRS

The Art & Heritage of Oregon Myrtlewood

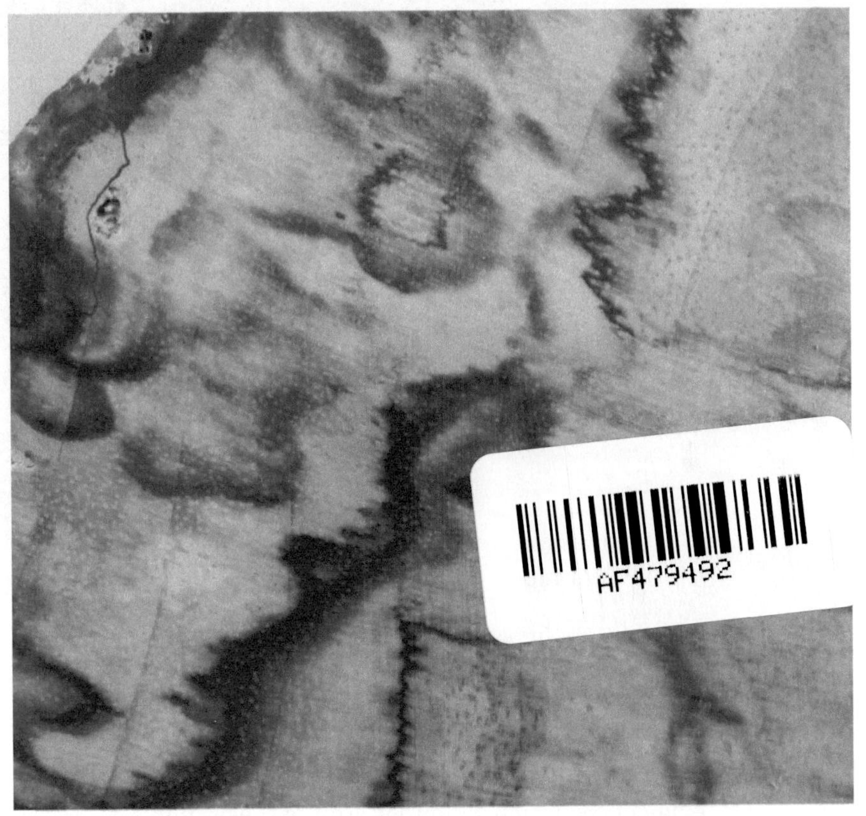

TERRY J. WOODALL

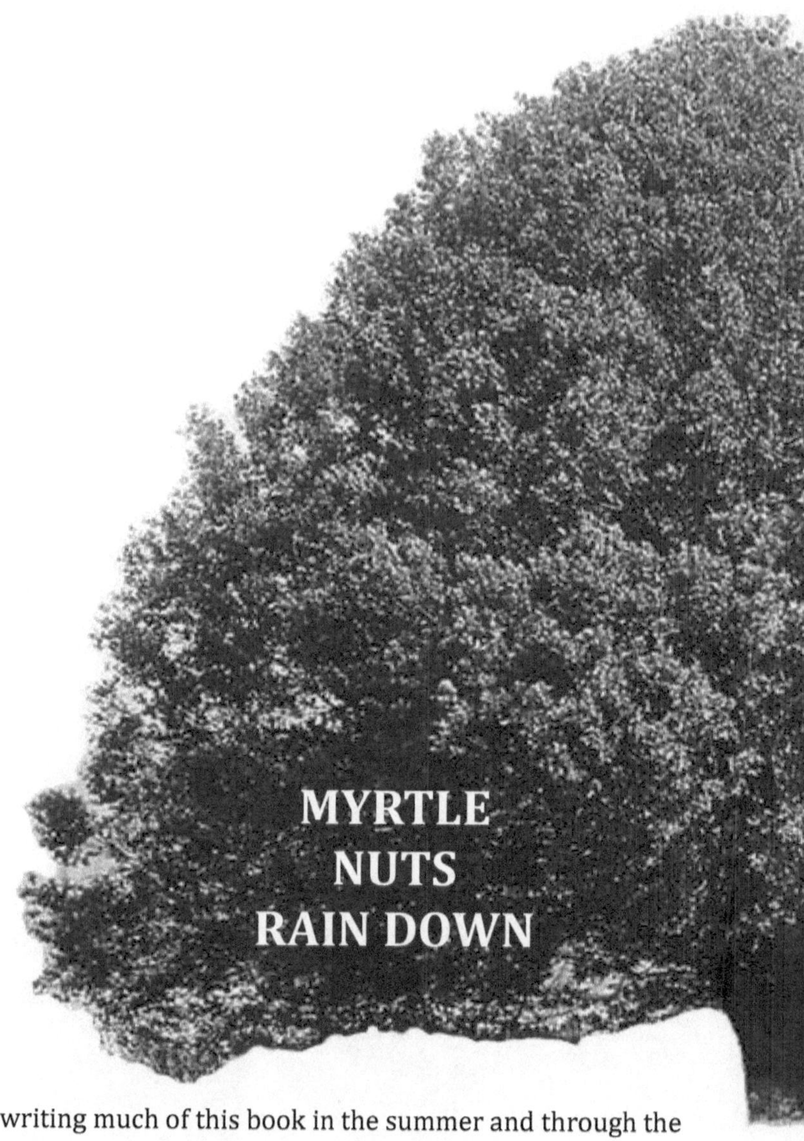

While writing much of this book in the summer and through the fall of 2021, myrtle nuts rained down unabated. Swelling voluminous with their thick, vegetative rinds, they mushed and crunched under foot. They coated my deck, driveway, and the ground everywhere the fertile branches could reach to drop their heavily laden loads.

Never before have I seen such a bumper crop of these spherical, marble-sized seeds, not even close, in my 40 years of dwelling under the domain of these same trees.

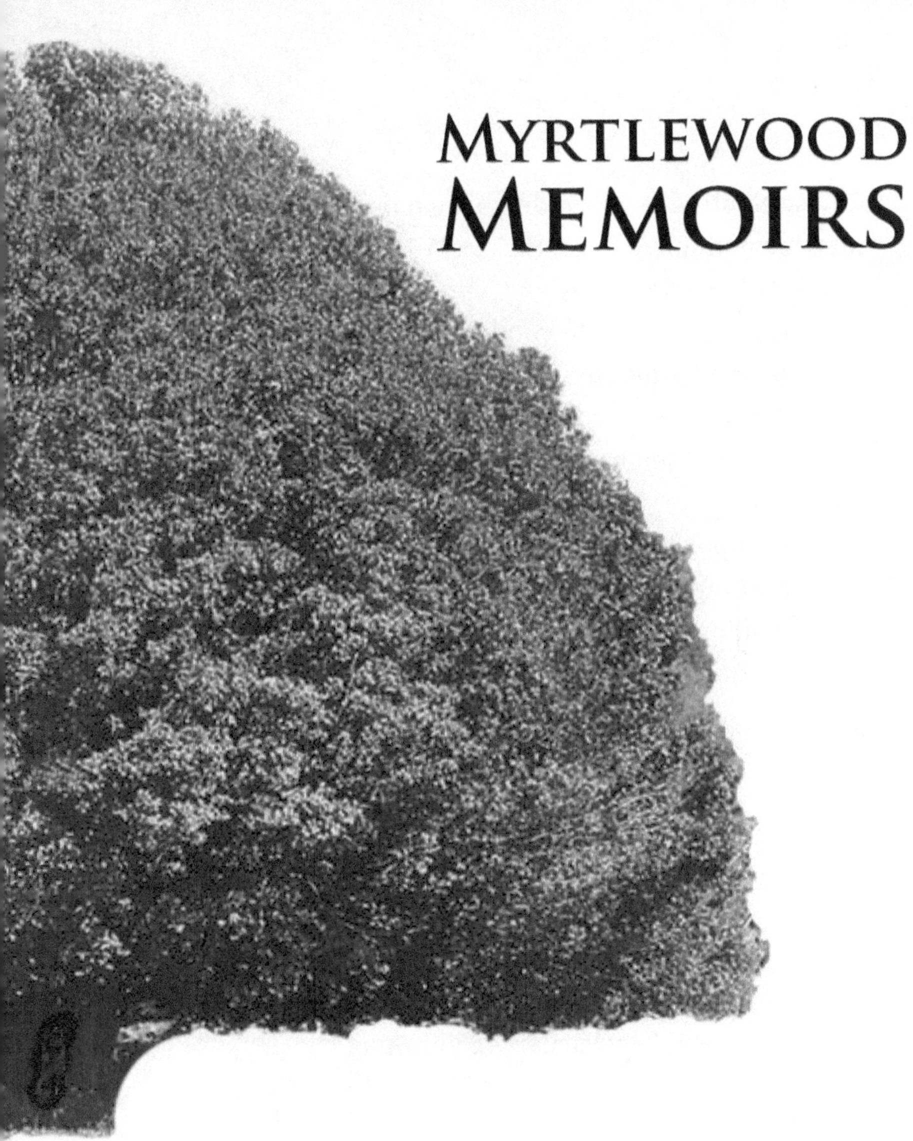

Myrtlewood Memoirs

Is it coincidental that this bountiful crop burst forth like a rain of poetic justice as this book took form? One can only wonder, and I am one who doesn't particularly believe in coincidences.

Yet the myrtle trees continued taunting me as they shed their tonnage of myrtle nuts, many larger than usual, putting a grand exclamation mark on their book of myrtlewood. And I'd like to think that things happen for a reason when the stars align in favorable ways.

TERRY J. WOODALL

Cover, "Spotted Owl," golden brown myrtlewood with black myrtlewood inlaid eyes, H17" x W11," by the author; background of myrtle leaves.

Page 1, ghost of myrtlewood past, "The Myrtlewood Man," natural wood grain image.

Page 2-3, immense myrtle tree of yesteryear, over 90' in breadth and height with a 10' diameter, photographer unknown.

Page 5, opposite, myrtle leaf fossil prints collected by the author from the Tyee formation, Southern Oregon. Dated at 50 million years by Southwestern Oregon Community College's geology department.

All photographs without credits are by the author.

ISBN 9798986146607

Published in 2022 by PacCarve Publishing
terrywoodall.wordpress.com | terrywoodall.com
Library of Congress Registration #TXu 2-327-344

Editing & Book Production:
Harvard Girl Word Services | harvardgirledits.com

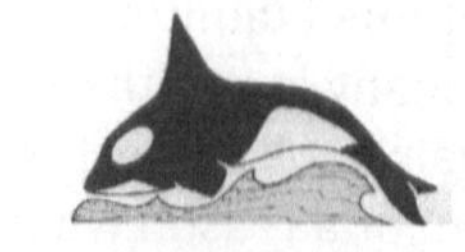

PacCarve Publishing

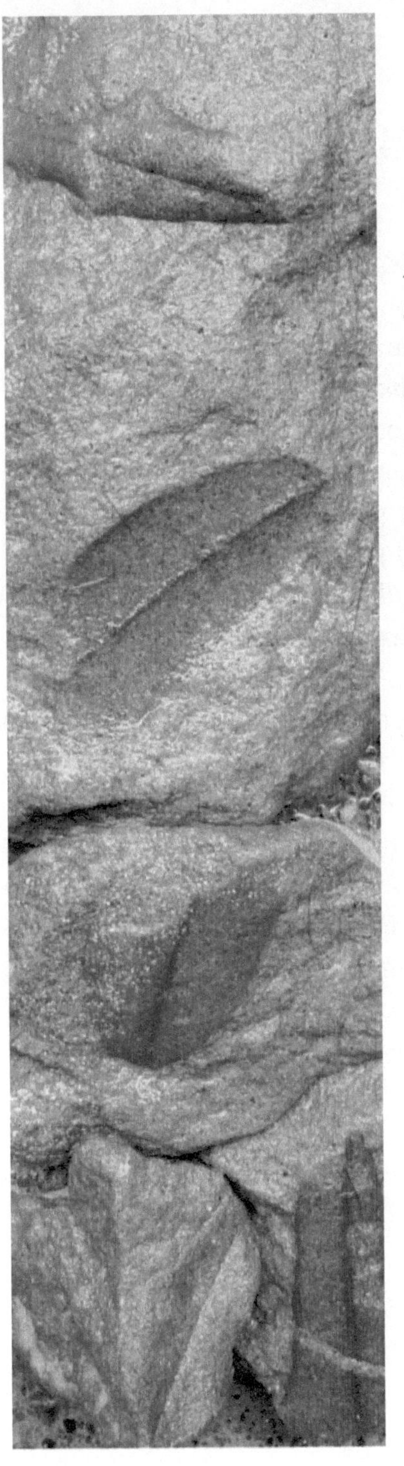

*In memory of my grand-
mother, Hilda "Tommy"
Thomas, who fascinated
me with her tales of
living and logging in the
back country of Southern
Oregon and gave me the
scent of my first myrtle
leaf when I was barely at
the age of remembering.*

FOREWORD

Myrtlewood contributed significantly to the aura of exotic resources of southwestern coastal Oregon. Stands of aromatic myrtles, towering Port Orford cedar trees, and magnificent "spruce clears" used for manufacturing airplanes were notable, regional forest products. In the early twentieth century these trees attracted loggers, manufacturers, purchasers, and promoters. Myrtlewood was touted as a unique resource found only in the "Holy Land" and in Coos, Curry, and Douglas counties. The tree produced an exceedingly hard wood that polished to a lustrous finish, often with intriguing colored swirls and burls.

Myrtlewood grew rapidly in popularity in the first decade of the twentieth century for paneling, furniture, novelties (bowls, boxes, dishes, trays, gavels, candlesticks), and carvings. In 1905, Coos County sent myrtlewood furniture for its exhibits in the Forestry Building of the Lewis & Clark Exposition in Portland. The exhibit area was paneled in fir and myrtlewood. In 1908 Louis J. Simpson, lumberman and founder of North Bend, used myrtlewood paneling and furniture in the entry hall of his mansion at Shore Acres, his seaside estate. The following year Carl A. Smith, owner of C. A. Smith Lumber Company in Bunker Hill, erected a three-story office building and had his private apartments paneled in myrtlewood.

In 1909, while visiting the Alaska-Yukon-Pacific Exposition in Seattle, President William Howard Taft heard about a remarkable myrtlewood table from Coos Bay displayed in the Oregon Building. "I want to see this wood," Taft said, and walked his party through the exhibits to the table "which he pounded with his big right fist while commenting on its beauty." In 1915, Coos County submitted a grand myrtlewood dining table and eight chairs designed by Wade Hampton Pipes, an arts-and-crafts architect in Portland, for the Oregon exhibits at the Panama-Pacific Exposition in San Francisco.

Exhibits featuring myrtlewood and its craftsmen nurtured and promoted this product growing in the river valleys of Oregon's southwest coast.

Myrtlewood sustained a regional "cottage industry." It became a business often carried on by in-home workshops manufacturing primarily for the tourist trade. Construction of Highway 101 in the 1930s stimulated the enterprise and led to opening of speciality myrtlewood stores offering numerous wares. For more than a century myrtlewood has sustained its appeal for shoppers and become a hallmark of a specialized forest product of Oregon.

Terry Woodall's consuming interest in making myrtlewood products and exploring its history is the subject of *Myrtlewood Memoirs: the Art and Heritage of Oregon Myrtlewood*.

His volume recounts the heretofore mostly undocumented story of crofting and carving myrtlewood and the magical attraction of this tree on generations of artisans and customers.

Stephen Dow Beckham
Pamplin Professor of History, Emeritus
Lewis & Clark College

ACKNOWLEDGMENTS

In the spirit of the non-fiction contract between writer and reader, all events and human interactions in this memoir are true, no matter how far-fetched they seem. Most short exclamations throughout these stories are exactly as they were spoken by the individuals described.

The many people contributing to these factual accounts and verifying the activities are greatly appreciated. There would not be a story without you. There also wouldn't be this book without all the myriad technicalities being worked out, and for this I owe a debt of gratitude to my editor and publishing manager Heidi Connolly and her Harvard Girl Editing Services.

I would like to thank Steve Grief for his research assistance in the Coos History Museum and Mike Erbele for taking the time for an interview. Also, Shaun Earle for photo layout and a wealth of advice, and Miladinka Milic for her excellent cover design.

Information comes from many sources, and for this I wish to thank Penny Humbert, Loreena Oerding, Ron Smith, Judi Larson, Jerald Humbert, Imogene Bechtel, and Carol Scoville.

Family support is always a necessity, beginning with my father, Roy Joseph Woodall, and my mother, Juanita Rose Parks, who forever encouraged me to express myself through writing. To my children, Astra, Joshua, and Maria, of whom I am so proud, and, above all, to my wife Carlin for going through the flames with me for this book, and emerging intact on the other side.

MYRTLEWOOD
MEMOIRS

TABLE OF CONTENTS

PROLOGUE

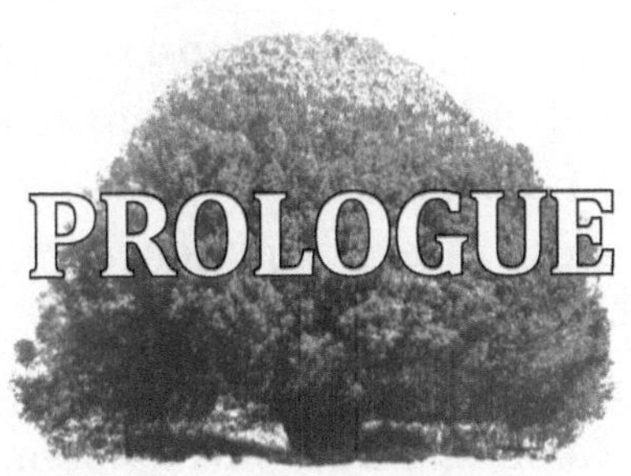

Myrtlewood: Our National Treasure Tree

Things of extreme value to humans often achieve the status of treasure, whether diamonds buried deep in the earth, or whale dung scattered on an ocean beach ("ambergris," worth $10,000 per pound). And where there is treasure, there are legends, myths, and magic fed by fervent imagination. Yet all, big or small, carry with them some basis of fact.

Mysteries from dense dark forests, like the lure of hidden gold or the elusive trail of Bigfoot, have ignited our imaginations with childlike wonder and intrigue throughout time. Apprehensions and fear of the wooded unknown only amplify the thrill of exploring deep into the wildwood to reveal its many secrets.

A rare forest denizen in all its furtive glory is our treasure here. From the fabled myrtlewood tree comes a forest gold, complete with its own aura of mystery expressed in its gnarled exterior growth and highlighted by the complex colors and grain patterns found within.

The southern end of Oregon's Coast Range mountains and the northwestern end of the Klamath Mountains contain prime habitat for myrtlewood stands. There are far more ridges in these mountains then actual peaks, miles of undulating spines with sheer canyons dropping off in all directions. If you tightly wadded up a sheet of paper, opened it up, and spread out the crinkles, this is what the topography of these ranges would look like: a maze of woods that seems to go on forever, a place where one could easily become disoriented and lost.

East and southeast of Oregon's Coos Bay, in the heartland of myrtlewood, the trees mix in a temperate forest of endless Douglas fir that blankets the slopes, which includes the tallest known Doug fir specimen on earth. Myrtle can be dense along creeks and rivers, thick along pastures and prairies, yet also creeps up mountainsides and scatters along canyons. It is not everywhere in these habitats, however, as alder dominates certain areas, and the never-ending fir forests lay claim to most wild, mountainside acreage everywhere in western Oregon.

The myrtlewood range of Southwestern Oregon, with its artists, craftsmen, and history-heritage, may not exist on any national treasure list, but as one of the rarest and most beautiful woods of the world, I assert that it is, nonetheless, without a doubt, a national treasure. After all, would the Grand Canyon be any less "grand" without its official designation?

On a trajectory toward National Treasure status, these written records take the reader through the early history of this tree and on to the eyewitness accounts of this artist/writer's path as it winds through myrtlewood country and into the world of wildlife art.

Enjoy the journey!

Reflections in a Myrtle Grove

It is a bright October evening with a hangover of summer, and I have come to this place unfettered, unlike some other times in my past. This is my chosen spot of homage...and why not? The pioneer spirits still watch over here as the gnarled, ancient trees stand sentinel and bear witness. I have recounted many struggles and uttered many sighs of relief in this wooded sanctuary, as well as celebrated accomplishments, all pertaining to wrestling objects of beauty from an icon of nature. I initiated this homage in another October years ago when a small sign reading "Hoffman Wayside" jumped out from the highway's edge and directed me into a magical riverside grove. That chance pilgrimage, which occurred while on a long route to newly found work carving wildlife for a myrtlewood factory, changed my life.

On this day, before lifting myself up from the flat and cold serpentine, I continue peering over the abrupt edge while lying as flat as the massive rock lies, peering into the deep green below, watching, watching...until finally they appear, their spawning streaks of red giving themselves away against the dark—salmon! Ripe with eggs and chasing their life courses upstream, salmon too big for the fisherman's ice chest, only fitting by folding them in half. Salmon, darting and circling and, to my delight, jumping clear of the river's surface and landing in great splashes. Immersed in this ageless ode of wild nature, my fingers feel the surface of the great stone pushing out over the river, polished smooth to a green shine by untold numbers of footholds pressing hard for the traction necessary to land these heavy fish.

A thousand years, perhaps even 10,000 years, of footprints have worn away the stone's mineral layers. Twenty feet in length and jutting up and out into the river, it's a natural power spot for the ancient spirit seekers and hunters of fish. When I finally rise, I can see the forks of two wild mountain rivers joining forces to take aim at the stone obstacle from a quarter mile upstream. Downstream from the forks and the immense boulder a series of wide, open lowlands slow the gushing mountain spill to a lazy ramble until it drowns in the Pacific Ocean 25 river miles away.

But this story isn't about the ageless geology beneath me or the salmon plying the river over the rock's edge. This story is about the trees at my back, the thick green mantle of the river that gulps up the flood plain's H_2O and nourishes multitudes of living entities, including the salmon and Native Americans and, eventually, the first pioneer settlers like Abe Hoffman, who arrived in 1853. Many of the myrtle trees here witnessed Hoffman's first log cabin planted amongst them, and snickered when flood waters swept it away in the homesteader's first winter.

These are not just any trees. These are one of America's most exquisite hardwoods, massed together and concealing a beautiful wood grain like no other. Oregon's myrtle is the sole member of the laurel family inhabiting the North American continent and lives only on its western edge.

Unraveling its secrets is my calling. It is the reason I pay homage here in admiration of these trees.

This sanctuary of myrtlewood shrouding the river counts as my personal salvation, since the wood it represents has provided for the honest work of a career needed to raise a family, and that drive is reinforced by every reflective visit.

Here, I lean into the hollow heart of an arboreal monarch and am surrounded by its burl-encrusted trunks.

Here, I follow the intertwined roots and branches snaking along the sandy river bank that interconnect with one tree after another. Here, I find the evidence of a national treasure tree wherever I look. And here, there, and everywhere, sylvan faces peer out like the wood gnomes of fairy tales and fingers of wood, like arrows on sign boards, point in random directions.

From the beginning, every visit kept me spiraling toward my destiny without stumbling on the inevitable spate of obstacles, and each sign urged me forward along the way.

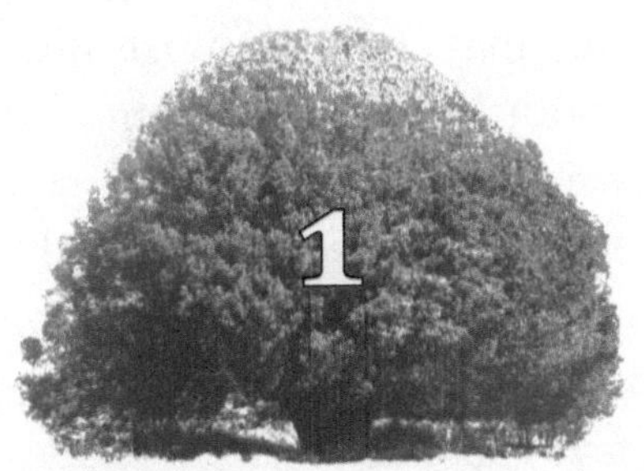

A Rose Is a Rose Is a Rose

By Any Other Name, It's the Same

What's in a name? The many monikers of myrtlewood are mostly due to its unique fragrance released upon breaking a leaf, a waft of pungent aromas from the camphor-like oils inside. Thus, its nicknames include spice tree, cinnamon tree, pepper tree, peppernut tree, sassafras laurel, balm of heaven, bay tree, and pepperwood.

Its most commonly accepted names are Oregon myrtlewood and California bay laurel, depending on what side of the Oregon-California border you stand. Other terms known to be used are California bay, California laurel, mountain laurel, pacific myrtle, bay laurel, California olive, or simply bay tree. No matter what you choose to call it, this is the same tree that's flourished in Oregon and California for over 50 million years.

Myrtlewood is categorized with its very own genus and species label, *Umbellularia californica*, and is the only tree in the laurel family native to North America. Its closest cousin is the *Laurus nobilis*, or common laurel, of the Mediterranean region, from which wreaths were made to adorn ancient Greek Olympians and Roman gods.

Pepperwood may be the most descriptive title of this tree with both its peppery scent and peppery grain patterns, known as tiger-stripe, that sometimes appear in the cross-section of a tree trunk. Sanding its wood and shredding its bark also releases strong scents from the oils within, aromas similar to liquorice, sometimes cinnamon, but almost always "peppery."

California Laurel (wider range) vs. Oregon Myrtlewood (denser stands)

In Latin, *umbella* translates to "parasol" and "sunshade," which helps us understand the term *Umbellularia* in the myrtle's genus name. *Umbellularia* describes the tree's small flowers that form an *umbel*, in botanical terms. An umbel is a number of short flower stalks equal in length that fan out from a mutual center point like the ribs of an upside-down umbrella.

We might even take this nomenclature one short step further to coin a new nickname, "the umbrella tree," to encompass all the names under the umbrella into one. Fitting all the numerous nicknames snugly under this umbrella would settle any variants pertaining to Oregon and California's many handles for the tree. In fact, my entire working life, and the work life of many others, has functioned under this hypothetical umbrella.

Myrtlewood is the universal name anointed to the wood itself and references to working the wood, whether in California or Oregon. Since the wood identity is firmly entrenched, we won't be sacrificing the myrtlewood name any time soon, especially when five different trees worldwide claim the same "umbrella tree" nickname. The myrtle tree stands alone, however, as the only tree in the world utilizing the scientific genus name *Umbellularia*.

In the myrtlewood realm, another questionable aberration of terminology can be seen in the common usage of the word "crofters" in place of the universal term "craftsman," a descriptor widely accepted and dating back to at least the 1930s. One enterprise of this era actually named their shop Duncan's Myrtlewood Crofters. The term *crofters* comes from Scotland, meaning one who has tenure and use of rural land, mostly related to farming. Early on, the main acquisition of myrtlewood for factories occurred as farmers cleared the entrenched groves to expand their arable lands. This overlapping relationship of farmers to woodworkers may help explain the origin of crofter in myrtlewood jargon.

Myrtle trees range from the Umpqua River of Southern Oregon down the coast to the San Bernardino Mountains of Southern California, and inland to the Cascade Mountains of Oregon and the Sierra Nevada range of California. Wood experts agree, however, that the range of the most desirable trees of highly figured wood grain stretches from Southern Oregon only into the vicinity of Mendocino, California.

Spanish Misnomer

Contrary to many early quotes of myrtle's being found only in Oregon and the Holy Land, this North American native is not related to the Old World common myrtle, *myrtus communis*, referenced in the Bible.

The *myrtus communis* tree, called *mirto* in Spanish, is native to southern Spain and other parts of the Mediterranean, including the Holy Land, and has been used for centuries for its culinary and medicinal properties. Soaps and perfumes integrate its extracted essential oils and dried leaves add an aromatic flavor to cooking. In parts of Southern Spain, where the leaves are used to help alleviate colds and bronchitis, it is still regarded as a symbol of love expressed by its use in bridal wreaths.

It was when early Spanish explorers sighted round, bushy trees on North American hillsides with a strong resemblance to their common *mirto* that they confused their new discovery with the myrtle of their homeland. Similarities in the strong, pungent scent of the leaves, due to the camphor-like oils found in both plants, made a strong case for an Eastern Pacific version of their smaller Mediterranean native.

From their early foothold on the western coast of North America, Spanish fleets established trade routes from Acapulco, Mexico to Manila in the Philippines. Regular trade routes were a northerly transit (east to west), and land was generally sighted in the vicinity of Cape Mendocino, California. They then followed the coastline south to Acapulco, their destination, with a return to Manila, following a southerly course. With their trade route down the California coast, the myrtles would mostly be observed in that state.

At least one ship found its way north to Oregon after being blown off course by storms and wrecking off the North Central Oregon coast in 1693. Called the Beeswax Wreck, the ship carried a cargo of beeswax destined for Spanish mission candles, and wax remnants are found by beachcombers in the vicinity of Tillamook, Oregon to this day. This crash landing of Spaniards on Oregon soil, however, occurred far north of any myrtle habitat.

With their long-term missions established in California, the Spaniards had plenty of time to get acquainted with the west coast myrtles, long enough that the name "myrtle" stuck. Future Californian botanists, by specifying the tree's actual lineage in the laurel family, encouraged the term California laurel. Evidently, Oregon continued using the name myrtle based on its first designation and usage by the Spaniards, and that moniker has persisted, becoming firmly established when Oregon Myrtlewood became more famous as a highly sought-after wood commodity.

Native Americans were myrtle's first practical users, as they consumed the tree's prolific round nuts, usually roasted or ground into a meal that could be pounded into flat cakes and sun dried for later use. The tree remains a desirable commodity due to its leaves, rife with a camphor-like oil that proves effective in repelling insects and in brewed herbal teas.

Native cultures also valued myrtle for its medicinal qualities and its role in ceremonial uses. Tossing myrtle foliage onto a fire was believed to drive away evil spirits in brush dance ceremonies. In the home, its leafy branches were burned as an agent against bad luck, its smoke ritually waved over those exiting to ward off harm. Branches were sometimes simply hung inside the houses for the same purpose. These California-based native cultures added an assortment of names in tribal tongues that identified the myrtle tree as *ba hem* (Pomo tribe), *wohkelo* (Yurok), *bahsa* (Southern Pomo) and *antcing* (Cahto).[1]

Earliest Woodworkers

According to an account from 1941, European craftsmen first identified the positive characteristics of myrtlewood for woodworking, placing the discovery of this high quality material for craftsmanship in the mid-1800s. As the story goes, a couple of Swiss brothers, part of the shipwrecked crew of a vessel grounded on the Oregon coast and skilled in wood carving, experimented with the unique wood, establishing for all future crofters its workability and essence of grain.[2]

The wreck of the Captain Lincoln off the Oregon coast in January of 1852 dovetails nicely with this story as everyone on board survived, a rare occurrence in such early shipwrecks. The schooner piled up on the beach two miles north of Coos Bay, Oregon, in the heart of myrtlewood country, leaving the marooned sailors and military dragoons to live in makeshift beach barracks for the next four months. Could the Swiss woodcarver brothers have been included on this ship's manifest?

Technically, this became the first white settlement on Coos Bay, the inhabitants even penning the name "Camp Castaway" for their modest shelter. By early spring, however, it was abandoned for the more established outpost of Port Orford, 60 miles to the south, which the men reached by traveling on foot.[3]

It is easy to speculate that the aforementioned wood-carvers stumbled across some driftwood of incredible grain patterns after spending time on a virgin beach near the mouth of an extensive myrtle tree watershed. After all, I have collected extraordinary specimens of myrtle driftwood in the very same vicinity a full 150 years hence. Whether the Swiss brothers were on this ship or another remains an unknown mystery, since verifiable sources have long ago melted into the mists of time.

North Bend Shipyards

Later in 1852, Coos Bay also came under the scrutiny of the lumber shipping magnate Asa Simpson, who, in his early years, plied the lumber trade between Astoria, Oregon and San Francisco. Shortly after exploring the bay, Simpson returned to chase the opportunities he had found there: a fine bay with access to thousands of acres of virgin timber. By 1856, Simpson had a sawmill operating at the current site of North Bend, Oregon's waterfront. To facilitate the shipping and sales of lumber, Simpson built his first ship in 1857, and 58 more in the next five years. Many impressive schooners were built to haul lumber, as well as the only clipper ship ever built on the west coast.[4]

Asa Simpson's shipyards on the bay at North Bend, with unlimited resources close at hand, built myrtlewood into many of their ships, including the ship's pilot wheel. No doubt a demand spread beyond North Bend for this prime hardwood of myrtle, which could be supplied from the Simpson shipyards where it was processed for the company's own use. As evidenced by Simpson, the earliest focus on utilizing myrtlewood for finer works came about with his shipbuilding enterprises.

A newspaper article from the 1920s states that myrtlewood found a purpose in the busy coastal shipyards, furnishing them with pilot wheels, interior finishing (galley and captain's stateroom), deck planking, and filled a score of other needs. "The polish it accrued after years of use made teak and mahogany look dull and unworthy, and many the old coastal skipper loved his myrtle-made pilot wheel because of its staunchness and beauty," claimed the newspaper. This hardwood that wears smooth without splintering served as the perfect element for windlass stocks, bits, chocks, jaws, cleats, and other specialties used in shipbuilding.

In 1904, Asa's son Louis, along with some partners, introduced the Coos Bay Furniture and Box Company, a venture that produced myrtlewood veneer from the exotic hardwood. If Asa was the worker bee turned empire builder, Louis became the inheritor son. Though more inclined to a lavish life style, Louis still managed to build and expand his father's holdings.

In fact, in 1902, Louis bought the small hamlet of Yarrow and the land surrounding it, and renamed it North Bend. His dream was to build the most important port and city north of San Francisco. After establishing the town, Louis added much to the growth of North Bend, all the while experiencing dramatic successes—along with tragic setbacks.

In a gain of personal luxury, Louis built Shore Acres, a stately mansion on cliffs overlooking the Pacific Ocean near the mouth of Coos Bay, and moved there in 1915. Well ensconced in the world of golden myrtlewood, he chose it to panel many interior walls and added fine myrtlewood furniture into the mansion layout. Sadly, in a string of tragic events that is said to have haunted him, the mansion burned down on July 4, 1921, three months after his beloved wife had died at the age of 50.

The First Myrtlewood Factories

An *Oregonian* newspaper article of the early 1920s provides us with a positive account and brief history of the myrtlewood industry in Coos County, Oregon:

It was in 1894 at the midwinter exposition in San Francisco that J.H. Hortsman, one of the oldest myrtle-

wood turners on Coos Bay, first saw cups made of the wood, being sold as curios. A year before that a man named J.B. Johnson, working at the Simpson sash and door factory, began turning the wood, but he gave it up as a bad job and became a shipbuilder. Hortsman was a woodworker with experience in Germany and was more persistent. In 1910 he began his experiments with the myrtle and he is still making beautiful articles from it at the North Bend Myrtle Wood Novelty Company.

Three factories in Coos County make practically all of the myrtlewood novelties that find their way to every part of the USA, the West Indies, Australia, Canada and the Pacific Islands. The largest of these is the Oerding Manufacturing Company of Coquille, organized by J.H. Oerding in 1907. Crofters were utilizing the wood much earlier, just not under the auspices of a "myrtlewood factory."

The second factory is a North Bend factory that was organized by E.A. Rose and the aforementioned J.H. Hortsman. Mr. Rose established the North Bend Myrtle Wood Novelty Company in 1915.

The third company is a flourishing factory in Marsh-field (in the old ironworks), that of Pomeroy, Duncan and Mehl, which began operation in 1911. The hands-on operator of the factory is Mr. E.D. Duncan.

This latter operation was located in the old ironworks building in Coos Bay. In 1937, a next generation Duncan built a new myrtle shop in North Bend, Duncan's Myrtlewood Crofters, which eventually became Bayview Myrtlewood Company and, finally, Myrtlewood Chalet.

Myrtlewood's Era of Opulence

The following quote is from "Myrtle Grows Along Roosevelt Highway," a pre-1930 newspaper article.

Older Myrtle specimens are large, gnarled, rambling branched giants, and it is from these trees that the beautiful wood is secured for furniture and table and desk ornaments. In former days, when this supply was larger, a great deal of hand turned furniture was made from the wood of the tree. For many years the furniture of the old Palace hotel in San Francisco was admired by connoisseurs from all parts of the world, who had seen the best and rarest of the period furniture of Europe. It had been all hand-made from Oregon myrtle. Unfortunately it was all destroyed in the San Francisco fire which followed the earthquake of 1906.

These descriptions from New York's *Frank Leslie's Illustrated Newspaper*, October 1875, are of the same hotel.

The furnishing of the hotel has been attended to in a style corresponding with the magnificence of the building. The greatest care has been given to selecting furniture, upholstery, table-ware, bed-clothing and everything necessary to throw the charm of a luxurious and refined home around the spacious rooms and stately halls. The workshops and warerooms of our own manufacturers and merchants have furnished many of the goods for the adornment of this great hostelry.

As we can see, the hotel's myrtlewood furniture orders went to local craftsmen. Just Imagine this era of opulence with craftsmen building cities and adding embellishments for all life's routines. Early appreciation of myrtlewood expanded with the opening of California's Palace Hotel in 1875. Even before that, though, in 1869, a golden spike pierced a railroad tie of polished California bay laurel (myrtle) in a ceremony celebrating the completion of the transcontinental railroad when the east and west lines met in Utah.

Early usages of the ubiquitous hardwood are vast, including interior finish work, organ construction, furniture, mathematical instruments, and walking beams for California oil well pumps. Farming tools of myrtlewood included everything from oxen yokes and plow beams to singletrees, and fuel for settlers rounded out many a basic pioneering need.

Conquering a hardwood, beginning with trees of the forest, and turning it into a thing of beauty and utility is not an easy task. The endeavor of crafting myrtlewood is significant, and this written record is a nod to all those who have gone before and established its importance for society's evolving culture. What did all these early entrepreneurs have in common? The recognition and appreciation for the inherent, valued potential of this wood resource, and proving that value well into the future. Many more discoveries and applications were yet to come.

...And Those Pioneer Spirits?

One-year-old Jemima Flett came to the Oregon Territory on an immigration wagon train from Winnipeg, Canada in 1842. Her parents died shortly after their arrival, leaving Jemima and her four sisters to be raised by sympathetic friends and relatives. Abraham Hoffman arrived in the Oregon Territory in 1850 from Indiana. At age 13, the orphaned Jemima married the older Abraham in the vicinity of Oregon City.

The Donation Land Law of 1850-55 was established to encourage settlement of the Oregon Territory, and Oregon claims were only granted at the federal land office in Oregon City. This land law was uniquely equitable in that it offered 320 acres to the husband and 320 acres to the wife of a married couple. Hoffman and his new bride submitted their claim for 640 acres sight unseen in a Southern Oregon wilderness that encompassed the merging forks of a wild river and the prairie and hills surrounding it.

The Hoffmans became man and wife in July of 1853 and, shortly after, pushed off into the unknown, traveling south to the burgeoning frontier town of Roseburg. After a day of following Indian trails to Camas Valley, they retired for the night, and continued through the Coast Range to their new homeland the next day. It was near the juncture of the middle and south forks of the Coquille River that they built their first log cabin and had established an official residence by 1854 in what is now the Hoffman Memorial Myrtle Grove state park.

The rains of their first winter had different plans for them, however, as recounted by a family descendant: "The river came up during the night, awakening them when water sloshed under their bed, and Abraham carried his young wife out of the cabin and they walked up to higher ground on the prairie and crawled into a haystack to ward off the pouring rain. At daybreak they watched the cabin float down the river with all their possessions."[5]

The Hoffmans, undaunted, regrouped to rebuild their second cabin nearby, but on higher ground. Their homestead lay two and a half miles upriver from a newly built military stockade that supported a few other homesteaders and was the beginning of the town of Myrtle Point. At this time, the fort was a frontier outpost facing miles and miles of mountain wilderness.

Rogue tribal wars against new settlers were erupting to the south in the mountains and canyons of the Rogue River, and tensions were running high among the local pioneers since the Coquille tribe was also restless and warring. Hence, another rudimentary stockade was built on the riverside near their cabin and on the edge of today's Hoffman Grove to hold so-called "unruly Indians." It wasn't long before a young Indian escaped, swam the river, and was killed by the time he reached the other side. The soldiers buried him there on the prairie. A few days later, a group of braves decorated with war paint came and danced around his grave as Jemima watched from her cabin. With the braves repeatedly pointing in her direction, a terrified young Jemima bolted the door, jammed a table up against it, and hid under the bed until Abraham returned home from his labor that evening.

A few days after this event, the Indians burned the stockade to the ground, along with the Hoffmans' cabin and all their winter supplies, sending the Hoffmans packing. The new settlers managed to escape back to Roseburg safely, where their first son was born in 1858. When Edward was six weeks old they returned to their land, Jemima on horseback holding the baby and Abraham on his feet walking at her side. Once again, not to be deterred, the Hoffmans erected yet another cabin and later operated a ferry for people and livestock to cross the nearby river.

When Jemima was just 21, after only eight years with her husband, Abraham died from a trek over the mountains to some gold mining fields. Left with three young'uns, Jemima Hoffman continued operating the ferry, feeding and housing weary travelers, and working the farm as best she could. Ed, the oldest son, continued working the farm, marrying in 1883 and raising a large family on the same homestead.

The family's livelihood, farming and logging of their land, consisted of falling huge conifers by hand saw and hauling them with teams of up to a dozen oxen. The logs were dragged to the river on plank skids, dumped in and floated to a mill in the town of Coquille. Along with log sales to the mill downriver, logging helped clear more farmland into the early 1900s. By 1914 the last of the heavy stands of myrtle had been cleared from the farm. Approximately 40 acres of flat land groves were opened to wood cutters to sell and use the wood gratis, in order to remove the trees to create more farm land.[5]

The grove bordering the other side of the river was spared, and today is the state park of Hoffman Memorial Myrtle Grove, one of the parkland sites of majestic Oregon myrtlewood trees. A bronze plaque dated 1949 and set on a large stone in the grove acknowledges the state park land donation from the descendants of Abraham and Jemima Hoffman.

[1]Skai Arbor, Julianne, *Tree Girl: Intimate Encounters with Wild Nature*, TreeGirl Studios LLC, 2017.
[2]Windsor, Nelle Rose, "The Story of Myrtlewood," the *News Press*, Coos Bay, Oregon, 1941.
[3]Gibbs, James A., *Shipwrecks of the Pacific Coast*, Binfords & Mort, Publishers, 1957.
[4]Beckham, Stephen Dow, Asa Mead Simpson, Lumberman and Ship-builder, *Oregon Historical Quarterly*, September, 1967.
[5]Palmer, (Hoffman) Nellie, *Remember When*, Myrtle Point Printing, Myrtle Point, Oregon, 1983.

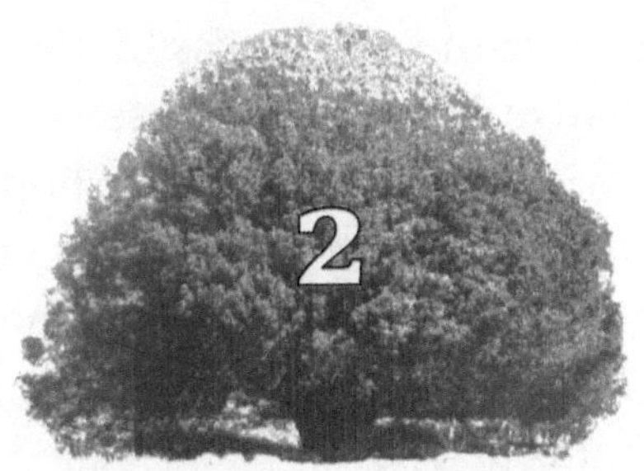

2

Myrtlewood Empires Rise & Fall

It was in the early 1900s that John Henry (J.H.) Oerding left Verona, North Dakota with his wife and 13 children to seek new horizons that would allow his family to expand its opportunities. In the Coquille Valley of Oregon he discovered a rich new underutilized resource.

J.H. Oerding came across a novel little shop where a craftsman named Mr. Fish (first name unknown) explored myriad new forms of myrtlewood, cutting and polishing marbled burls for unique table tops, revealing new discoveries and bringing to light unknown mysteries in wood grain. Mr. Fish also whittled canes by hand that added to his myrtlewood offerings.

Oerding was awestruck. These were the first myrtlewood objects he had ever seen created. Living on the edge of an expansive, fertile valley, he saw fields being cleared by farmers, with felled myrtle trees exposing rich grain at the cut ends. As he discovered the myrtle's abundance throughout Coos and Curry counties in this new land his mind was soon made up. He had found his calling, as well as an occupation for all his seven sons. The Oerdings would become myrtlewood crofters!

Intrigued with the craft possibilities of the beautifully grained native hardwood, the senior Oerding began his enterprise with a small woodcraft shop just across the Coquille River Bridge at the edge of the growing town of Coquille. This humble operation of 1907 quickly expanded into a progressive myrtlewood factory, the first of its kind, named J.H. Oerding and Sons.

A pair of spiraling candlestick holders turned about 1910 in that same small myrtlewood shop on the banks of the Coquille River became an heirloom of Ida Oerding, one of John Henry's daughters. Among several employees at that time was a German wood craftsman, and it was he who turned the spiral candlesticks "which proved what could be done with myrtlewood when properly aged and skillfully handled," according to Miss Oerding in *The World Newspaper* (Coos Bay, Oregon, May 21, 1970), adding, "It is from this successful experiment that the industry which is a major Oregon Coast tourist attraction and supplies a nationwide gift market has grown."

It turns out that J.H. Oerding wasn't the only one infatuated with myrtlewood and its products. Not long after the Oerdings began producing myrtlewood items, the noted writer Jack London arrived in Coquille seeking to have myrtlewood furniture specially made for his "Wolf House," a new home being constructed in Northern California. London and Oerding discussed the possibilities while sitting on the porch of the downtown Baxter Hotel.

The lack of machinery necessary for making Jack London's special furniture dampened Oerding's commitment, but London persisted, countering the myrtlewood master with a deal hard to refuse: London would purchase the needed machinery provided Oerding would produce his proposed furniture. They agreed on a deal, Jack London got his furniture, and the Oerdings acquired new machinery to expand their factory offerings.

In another turn of fate, Jack London's Wolf House burned down in 1913 just before it was to be inhabited. On a more positive note, the myrtlewood furniture was saved, as it had not yet been moved into the house. The Jack London State Historic Park in Glen Ellen, California still displays an occasional table from that original furniture, with other pieces in storage and some dispersed after the fire, current whereabouts unknown.

In 1919, the Oerdings built a new and more modern sawmill to help supply the myrtlewood factory. Named the Oerding Hardwood Sawmill, it featured a Yates band saw powered with large electric motors, a first in the area. Back at the factory site, they manufactured myrtlewood furniture and utilized turning lathes for bowls, plates, trays, lamps, and many other novelties and accessories. Selling and shipping their products throughout the USA during and after the First World War, the myrtlewood business boomed until J.H. needed to employ a dozen turners in his plant.

With a new marketing plan, Oerding Hardwood originated the idea of attaching a descriptive logo to the bottom of each item they produced. It may be hard to imagine this as a bold new idea, since applying a logo sticker to products has become so common place throughout the industry over its history, yet this is where it all started. The very first descriptive phrase on a logo applied to a line of myrtlewood products read "The most beautiful of beautiful woods."

According to the *Coquille Valley Sentinel*, Charles, one of the seven Oerding brothers, stated, "A man named Heath came to visit, and was so impressed that he asked for samples to take with him back east. Before long we were overwhelmed with more wholesale orders then we could accommodate."

In the early 1920s, an Oerding representative traveled to New York City and returned with orders for cigar boxes and stands for electric lamps for one of the most famous Fifth Avenue gift shops and myrtlewood candy boxes for a well-known candy maker. The Oerding factory continued its success making radio cabinets, book ends, courtroom and lodge gavels, cribbage boards, candy jars, shields for mounting antlers, large flower and small bud vases, vase-style lamps, powder boxes, smoking sets, nut bowls, and more from the golden wood.

By 1935, that first myrtlewood factory was renamed The Myrtle Burl and remained an Oerding family business, operated by them until it closed in 1989. In that year, and much to the chagrin of Coquille residents, the state bypassed the town with a new loop highway, dooming the last Oerding myrtlewood gift shop from a lack of business access. Before the bypass, I myself supplied carvings to Robert Oerding, son of Charles and the third-generation myrtlewood operator. Robert personally showed me around the shop, proudly pointing out his favored work, a line of fine-grained myrtlewood gunstocks.

The Torch is Passed

In its early times, the Oerding operations had led the myrtlewood industries of Southern Oregon from the inland town of Coquille, but in 1929 a new force vied for the leading role in myrtlewood popularity. A quaint and humble little house appeared on the coast highway in the seaport town of Marshfield advertising itself as The House of Myrtlewood. The iconic-sounding name evoked a noble sophistication, echoing the House of Lords or other regal titles of Old England, providing the modest shop a leg up to become the main destination landmark among all the others.

Imagine the excited anticipation of a grand opening. In a welcoming gesture by the owner, William Beaumont, the shop's solid myrtlewood doors were thrown open for the first time. The inside walls and counters shone with the golden wood, providing a fitting backdrop for all their products. This was a gift shop inside a house whose interior spilled over with creations of myrtlewood finery and embellishments for the home.

A large sign in the rounded shape of the myrtle tree extended out from the side of the building providing visibility from the highway in both directions. The word "Myrtlewood" dominated the middle of this original sign, followed by "Beaumont Wood Specialties." Another tree-shaped sign of the same size broadcast "The House of Myrtlewood" from the curbside. The slogan "The House of Myrtlewood, at the sign of the Myrtle Tree" appeared on the advertising brochures, and fully grown myrtle trees spread out from all sides of the "house," creating a fitting backdrop to the enterprise.

A separate facility in a different locale supplemented this gift shop building, producing the many products from, according to their brochure, "the largest and best equipped myrtlewood factory on the coast, and the only one making furniture as well as novelties."

This tree-shaped sign would remain the iconic symbol of the House for the duration of its history. Time passed. The establishment changed hands and locations, ultimately relocating to the other end of town, now renamed from Marshfield to Coos Bay.

This new location was large enough to accommodate both a factory and gift shop under the same roof since it had once been a door and sash factory. In 1972, Les Streeter came along, purchasing the myrtlewood business and expanding the building in all directions, including a second-floor addition. One well-known specialty that came from Streeter's new directives was golf club heads procured by many celebrities over the years.

Les was not only amiable and easy with conversation, but witty, a born salesman. With wavy hair that matched the silvery, curly, fiddle-back grain often found in myrtlewood, he fit the role of a true myrtlewood mascot as he championed his newfound resource.

Under Streeter's direction, the House of Myrtlewood encouraged visitors by offering tours of the factory where they could watch items being created. Along with a fudge bar for refreshments, coastal tee shirts and coffee mugs added selections to the gift shop. Unsurprisingly, the fudge bar became a particular favorite in this myrtlewood mecca.

From the mid-80s onward, my own sea life carvings occupied a space on the House of Myrtlewood shelves. On one special delivery of my work, I'd followed a busy crowd into the gift shop. A tour bus had emptied out, and the House was straining under the influx of new enthusiasts. I was just in time to hear one portly lady cry out above the melee, "I found an owl!" Beaming with triumph, she raised her prized carving above her head for all to see.

I squeezed through the bedlam with a box of carvings, and Les ushered me towards the counter. I had my father, affectionately known as "Dad Roy" Woodall, along for his first visit to the House of Myrtlewood, and introduced him to Les. "Be sure to visit our fudge bar," Les said with twinkling eyes, smiling his encouragement. "You'll have to try it—it's how we use up all the myrtle sawdust from the shop. We bake it into the fudge!" Dad Roy balked and rapidly backed up raising his hands. "Maybe some other time!" he said, and quickly reverted to queries about the myrtlewood business.

Les Streeter's daughter Tricia took the reins of the family establishment in the last segment of its operation, adding "Oregon Connection" to the House name. In 2006, the Star of Hope, a local community non-profit, purchased the business and operated it for 12 years.

In 2018, after 89 years of continuous operation, the flagship of myrtlewood shops retired its sign, closed its doors, and sold off its machinery. Ironically, the banner name Star of Hope has replaced the stoic House of Myrtlewood signage, since that non-profit continues warehousing their vehicles and supplies on the grounds of what was once one of the most influential myrtlewood shops of modern times. "Wait—come back!" the Star of Hope sign seems to plead, a stark reminder of the fading legacy of Oregon myrtlewood shops.

Spiritual Symbolism

Interestingly, that twist of fate from the Spanish misnomer of "myrtle" encouraged an avalanche of myrtlewood products based on biblical lore. At least five verses in the Bible mention myrtle, generating the magical mantra that myrtle grows "only in Southern Oregon and the Holy

Land." This tenet took hold early in myrtlewood's history, and as it grew legendary, the long shadow cast by those biblical quotes only added to the tree's mystique and the desirability of its wood.

It was not uncommon for shops to claim myrtle's "Oregon and the Holy Land" roots in labels and brochures, and to reference one particular verse in the Bible that read "Instead of the thorn shall come up the fir tree, and instead of the brier shall come up the myrtle tree." (ISAIAH 55:13)

References to the myrtle of Palestine only grew with time and behooved crofters to produce an abundance of myrtlewood items catering to churches and religious followings. Aside from the obvious crosses, large and small and of varying styles, we saw more and more applicable works: Greek fish with inscriptions, carved praying hands and Madonna figurines, candlestick holders, collection plates and bowls, communion trays, chalices, and altars of various sizes.

Symbolism built into an object equates to powerful objects, ones that channel and reinforce beliefs, and this occurred when crofters combined this fine wood with religious applications. In their 25 years of operation, G & B Myrtlewood, on the east side of Coos Bay, based much of their wholesale business on supplying churches across the nation with offering plates, crosses, and other adornments.

The small town of Myrtle Point, Oregon still leads the way with myrtle and the gospel, boasting the only church known to be completely paneled with myrtlewood throughout its sanctuary, with adornments of crosses and altars crafted from the same trees. Admirably, churches have made widespread use of this glorious natural material, regardless of the tree's roots and biblical references, all the while providing a huge boon to the myrtlewood industry.

Monumental Myrtlewood Furnishings

It was under the guiding hand of Samuel Boardman, the first supervisor of the Oregon State Parks Department, that one myrtlewood project of Herculean proportions took shape. Boardman, who took the position in 1929, became inspired by the rustic furniture of Timberline Lodge on Mount Hood about the same time that two enormous myrtle logs were gifted to him on the southern-most area of the Oregon Coast.

Boardman had just opened a new lodge at Silver Falls State Park, which lies in the Cascade Range mountains east of Salem, the capital city of Oregon. Since he had acquired the land and established this jewel of a park, Boardman envisioned the use of the myrtle logs to help furnish the lodge in a rustic style similar to Timberline's furnishing. Linking all his inspirations together, he aggressively pursued his new pet project.

Boardman sought the advice of local myrtlewood crofters and proceeded with a plan for tables, chairs, and benches to grace the newly constructed lodge. He also enlisted Margery Hoffman of the Oregon Arts Project to design the furniture and provide the dimensions and details for construction. Hoffman was the designer of the furnishings at Timberline Lodge, which had first caught the attention of the park's chief.

On the road-less side of the Chetco River, seven miles inland from the town of Brookings, lay the two logs of 5' diameters and fully 40' lengths. What to do with this challenging situation?

The gifter of the logs, Elmer Bankus, accomplished the first task of moving the behemoths across the river and to an accommodating sawmill, which turned out to be a one-horse operation described by Boardman as a "teapot mill." The park chief trusted the one-man operator to get the job done, however, and submitted the required dimensions of cut lumber. "How he ever handled these logs and produced the requested lumber will always be a mystery to me," Boardman wrote in a description of the process.

The end result of prime myrtlewood planks and boards supplied the lodge with 25 tables, 82 chairs, 11 fireplace benches, and a large dining room bureau. These pieces would sit well in a hall of Vikings, as one large table top consisted of two planks a full 3" thick. The benches and chairs that complemented the tables were of a similar heavy construction.

According to a description of this myrtlewood venture by the Oregon Parks and Recreation Department, the green and raw-cut lumber weighed 18,000 pounds before it entered experimental dry kilns at Oregon State College (now known as Oregon State University) and 8,000 pounds at the end of the drying procedure. That's a lot of moisture content! It took a full year after the lumber had been moved by trucks to a Works Progress Administration shop in Portland before workers transformed it into the impressive furniture still in use at the lodge.

The Silver Falls timeline began with the establishment of the Silver Falls State Park in 1933; the building of its lodge in 1940; and the lodge furniture completed and installed by 1945.

In an interesting side note on a darker version of carving, Boardman put forth the idea of a "carving unit" at Silver Falls as an educational deterrent to people's tendencies to carve on picnic tables, trees, and other park properties. Starting with carved initials and on to the trysting tree, these most blatant expressions of our identities have always been with us. Think of those hand prints etched on Stone Age cave walls that cry out, "I was here!"

The planned enclosed carving unit would enable unlimited graffiti-like activities on designated wood structures. Perhaps in the back of his mind, the park supervisor did not want to see his valuable myrtlewood furniture damaged in the future. The wooden centerpiece meant for sanctioned wood desecration never progressed past the planning stages, however, and the furniture, fortunately, remains in good condition to this day.

Myrtlewood Furniture of a Modern Era

At one time, old general stores were ripe for conversion into shops and galleries on the Oregon Coast. With its old-fashioned gas pumps and false-fronted structure, one of these multipurpose businesses at the south end of Coos Bay even boasted a stout iron post and ring for hitching up horses. When it's time of usefulness waned, it became Heritage Myrtlewood, claiming a long and soulful niche in the lineup of myrtlewood establishments and hosting a more modern-era production of myrtlewood furniture brought about in the 1990s.

Chuck and Georgianne Alcock, a husband-and-wife team who ran a myrtlewood factory and shop in Grants Pass, Oregon, also had a firm anchor in Coos Bay as owners of Heritage Myrtlewood. For many years the Alcock's ran the shop that faced a busy Highway 101. Near the end of their run with Heritage Myrtlewood, Chuck put together a grand slam of fine furniture production, working out an agreement with an oak furniture component manufacturer named Bentwood Furniture, also operating in Grants Pass.

Chuck Alcock was duly seasoned with myrtlewood design and applications well before taking on the special furniture production. He followed his plan of constructing furniture elements, posts, and faces that he fully laminated from myrtle strips, which were then tooled in the versatile oak factory. After the tooling, the multi-colored and contrasting strips of myrtlewood jumped out in a maze of wood grains. The end product resulted in some of the most outstanding natural grain furniture imaginable.

Due to this mass production setup for creating wood components in quantity, furniture could be assembled on a large scale, giving way to entire bedroom sets, expansive dining tables and chairs, hutches, and luxurious living room appointments. This eye-popping showcase of fine furnishings filled up the Heritage shop with a smorgasbord of myrtlewood for quite some time.

I will forever be grateful to Georgianne Alcock, who always showed generosity toward me, purchasing my carvings even in the off-season when tourism business slowed. Chuck was also quick to share with others anything new he came up with, from technology to products, rather than hoarding his trade secrets. Both Chuck and Georgianne gave me sound business advice, and backed another myrtlewood animal carver of natural talent who inspired me as I progressed.

Ron Foster, another Grants Pass dweller, had a knack for creating realistic animals, and fully captured their "look." Ron's unusual quirk, albeit forgivable, was that he avoided applying finishes for the final step of his carvings. Orders for his work were sent out in raw, fresh-carved wood to the receiving shop, which then applied its choice of finish.

The Alcock team was well respected in the myrtlewood realm of businesses, but all good things meet an end. After a time, their furniture production with the Bentwood Company fell through and eventually Heritage Myrtlewood evaporated as well. The old general store went on the market, never to become a myrtlewood shop again.

Myrtlewood Makes Good Money

In the early history of North Bend, Oregon, making your own money became a literal reality when the city council voted to produce its own coins from local myrtlewood. The varied color tones of the wood-turned-to-coins, with attractive engravings on both sides, immediately became popular and widespread in use. A local newspaper ad encouraged townspeople to "Bring your money to us," with the slogan "Myrtlewood Money is good Money!"

It is not surprising that this renegade currency became implemented when banks were falling like dominoes during the Great Depression. Many communities, including North Bend, had to rely on scrip, and invented novel substitutes for legal tender.

After the first $1000 circulated in 1933 without any problems, a second issue of $1000 was released, all in five denominations ranging from $.25 to $10 tokens. The city guaranteed the new money with a surety bond, and planned to fully redeem the myrtlewood coinage when the financial crisis had passed and the only bank in town reopened. Coin collectors and souvenir hunters created a demand for the mintage, however, and local popularity of its use continued. Although the currency value was limited to the city of North

Bend, interest in the scrip spread to the point where Chase National Bank of New York placed a full issue of the coins on public display in their coin collection. Today's owners of collections are spread far and wide, and full sets of the coins are rare; in fact, fewer than 10 are believed to exist.

Due to the lack of populace participation after several appeals, city officials gave up on trying to redeem the new money, finally announcing that the token coins would remain in circulation as legal tender for perpetuity. To this day, the myrtlewood money is solvent and can be redeemed for cash by the city, although, given collectors' inflated value, that rarely happens. After all, this money, literally grown on trees, is now of antique quality, highly prized for the limited numbers produced. Myrtlewood is the only wood still in use as a base "metal" for legal tender.*

North Bend's Depression Issue Myrtlewood, Patricia Choat Pierce, P & G Productions, North Bend, Oregon, July, 1993.

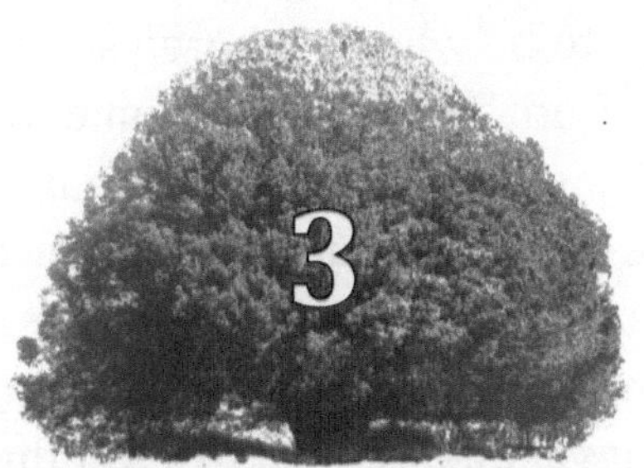

Myrtlewood Lantern Lights the Way

In 1974, I found myself with a new bride in an old pickup truck, scouting around for land on which to live and myrtlewood to feed my career dreams. My young wife Carlin, partly city girl and mostly country gal, loved being near the sea, all of which suited me just fine. During this venture, she also fell in love with the funky seafaring town of Charleston, Oregon.

That old truck, a 1949 GMC behemoth, carried more iron in its bumpers than found in most small cars today. Driving steady and sure, as long as you held the gear shift lever firmly in place, the GMC carried us from the interior Umpqua Valley, across the Coast Range mountains, and all the way down to the Oregon coast.

After we reached the coastline, a side road took us along the south arm of Coos Bay, where a scattering of modest wood houses held their own against the daily tidal surges. Some of these houses appeared to have landed in the mud flats as if they dreamed of becoming houseboats, and I pulled up to a stop at one of these brave dwellings. An older man, tall and weathered, strode out.

Frank was a kindly soul, content with life as many seafarers seem to be when anchored solidly on shore, and had emerged from his bay-side home with an amiable greeting. In this part of the world, the heavy salt air that hung over the bay challenged the sun at every turn, and only the powerful north winds of summer were capable of pulling back the curtains of stubborn fog. Three substantial myrtlewood logs shone weathered silver through this misty sunlight as it engulfed Frank's place, and that's what had given me pause to park in the grassy field that served as his front yard. The logs, peppered up and down with outcrops of burls, promised spectacular grain patterns from the wood within.

When I made some polite queries about the status of said logs, Frank rose to the occasion. "I rounded up those logs way out at sea with my fishing boat," he proudly asserted, "although they were the long stem of one tree that we reeled in. Who knows how long that myrtle tree bobbed around out in the ocean, but once we had it on shore we trimmed it into these three logs."

Frank actually seemed more interested in showing us some nice long-neck clams that he had recently excavated from his backyard, and led us towards his house. "You can't eat myrtlewood," he commented matter-of-factly, as he commenced to explain all the methods of acquiring and preparing the shellfish morsels for the table. Then, most generously, he bagged up some of his prizes from a bucket on his back porch, kindly bestowing them upon us for our later use.

Eventually I nudged Frank back to the subject of those sparkling silver-gray myrtle logs. I explained that I had a crosscut saw and would be forever indebted if he would allow me to saw a slice of burl off the side of one log. He was more than happy to accommodate my youthful zeal, and soon we'd found an accessible section that I could cut on. This entailed hand sawing with a 4' long, large-toothed saw. It took two solid hours of labor, which I timed, but when I finished cutting, I had a sizable slice of prime myrtlewood. In this time of my humble beginnings, a labor-saving chainsaw remained out of reach and a distant goal.

In my mind, this challenging task heralded back to my great grandfather who'd felled and bucked conifers with crosscut saws in the early logging era. Acquiring raw material in such a fashion gave me a renewed appreciation of his life of labor.

The horizontal cut that fell from the side of the log curved around the exterior burls to form a natural edge of varied contours, and maintained an average width of 12" across the freshly sawn surface. Another major factor determined the shape and look of this 4' long hardwood slab. The section of log anointed for cutting happened to be the very butt end of what once was a stalwart tree of the forest. It is fairly common for a myrtle tree to be hollowed out from decay where it meets the earth, and such was the case with this one, causing the wood surface of my cut to be indented slightly in the middle where it was beginning to meet the decayed hollow. Here, striking colors and contrasts were revealed as the good wood met the encroaching decay.

Black, tan, yellow, and gray all swirled together inside this cross view, while the exterior remained the silver gray patina from weathering. A straw-colored field merged into yellows, then bands of black, intoned with silver grays, and finally, the indented center peppered with white speck that created a honeycomb effect. In a moment of amazement, I recognized a solitary human-like figure outlined in the grain pattern. The image covered a full two-thirds of the myrtlewood slice on its flat, interior surface.

Upon returning to our modest home from Charleston, we savored our cache of clams and I laid out the myrtlewood treasure from the sea. On the front porch that served as a workshop, using the luxury of a power belt sander, I sanded it smooth in a fit of unrestrained anticipation. There, unmistakable in the fine wood grain, an image similar to a Chinese silk screen character appeared that resembled an old man hunched over and holding up a lantern.

Coos Bay Wagon Road is a backwoods route connecting the interior valley to the coast. True to its name, the road once hosted regular stagecoach runs. New highways have left it remote and semi-abandoned, although it is still maintained for logging access. This hidden-away road beckoned as another exploratory route for my old GMC truck, and so we began our new foray to the coast from the inland Umpqua Valley.

Negotiating the wagon road took us from east to west through the coastal mountains, where the track eventually dropped down from the higher elevations into the Coquille River drainage. The Coquille (commonly pronounced "co-key-el") boasts Oregon's largest watershed of rivers that begin their journey in the coast range, and consists of five main stems with many tributaries, all rich with myrtle. Following the banks of the East Fork Coquille, these myrtle trees began to appear, and numerous modest-sized water-falls spilling over river boulders were in sight of the road. Middle East Fork Falls was the largest and most impressive of these falls, causing us to immediately pull over to savor our wild nature discoveries.

As I nosed the old pickup along and traversed what is known as Brewster Canyon, a gravel spur forked to the right and, shortly after that, an old general store loomed up out of the mist to the left. It was the first hint of civilization and the only building we'd encountered in the past 40 miles of gravel road, so I instinctively pulled up beside it and stopped. This must be Sitkum, I thought; it appeared that the general store/post office remained the only building of the town proper. Scattered ranches and scant residencies populated the rest of the small Sitkum prairie, surrounded by mountain ridges in every direction that formed the geological rarity of a completely boxed-in valley.

An old man hobbled out of the store, the proprietor, no doubt, and I asked him about the myrtle forests hereabouts. He puffed up with pride and insisted on showing us around, relishing the opportunity to talk about his hidden-away valley. Expounding on its ice age geology, he pointed out nearby peaks that climbed 1500' above the valley floor and explained how they got where they were, with many references to glaciation.

"Where you from?" he finally inquired.

"The Umpqua Valley," I said, "we just came over the wagon road from Reston."

"No—where do you live?" he prodded.

"A place called Dillard, in the South Umpqua Valley. A major flood hit recently, made a mess out of everything in the lowlands."

"Never heard of it, but we had our share of flooding. Let me show you something," the old fella added with glee. We proceeded around the corner of his establishment that faced towards the river and he swept out his arm. "This is what the flood did here. Piled up all these myrtle trees."

At least a dozen stems of myrtle trees were jammed up helter-skelter, long and true trunks with a medium diameter of about 12" showing through the tangle. "They're easy to get at and you can have all you want of them," he offered, brimming over with goodwill. Of course, he may have been looking for an easy clean-up, but I took it as gesture of kindness. Any way you looked at it, what lay before us was a bonanza of myrtlewood left by the receding floodwaters. I was bewildered at the sight of so many accessible myrtle logs, which were so close, yet sadly, so far from the reach of my current capabilities. I could have happily salvaged the wood a decade later after I had acquired substantially more equipment, but not on this day.

As we bid farewell, the kindly country gent suggested that we visit a nearby myrtle preserve. According to his directions, we backtracked a short distance to the fork we had passed, and proceeded up Brummit Creek Road. Within a few miles, it became obvious that we were on the right track.

To the north and at the base of peaks rising up 2000', a lush rain forest spilled out with a canopy of resplendent trees. These myrtle giants stood sentinel at the location of the myrtle preserve, while the east fork of Brummit Creek meandered through and soaked their hungry roots.

With a careful surveillance of the thick myrtle groves lining the creek, we cruised slowly up the gravel road until we spied a reddish, derelict sign nailed to a 3' wide myrtle bole. In barely discernible lettering weathered away throughout the years, I made out the following designation: "Oregon Myrtle Preservation Area, through the Cooperation of the Bureau of Land Management and the Save the Myrtle Wood League." Green moss grew around the edges of this sign, which had shifted into a slanting pose over time, but, luckily, the bullet holes that are a typical fate suffered by rural signage were absent.

There wasn't any other fanfare, as this remote location boasted nothing more than a mountain wilderness environment. It was a comfort to know that all these old growth myrtles extending before us for many acres were in an official state of preservation. Subtle as these groves seemed when blended with the thickly forested mountain realm, I knew this to be a place of importance, and a place to revisit.

Although there was no other sign designation, further research revealed that this site had become Maria C. Jackson State Park through the efforts of Save the Myrtle Woods, Inc. The merger into the state park system occurred in 1946, and the remote site still remains undeveloped.

Shifting gears into an upgrade, the old truck became a plain white VW van converted into a homemade camper that qualified as a garden variety hippie van due to its bright yellow, sunflower-patterned curtains. Our "magic bus" engendered more coastal outings, and even furthered its reach with an adventure to Veracruz, Mexico.

Courtesy of our traveling wonder, we ventured along another back road, where a quaint hamlet, aptly named Riverton, appeared, hugging the banks of the wide and placid main stem Coquille River. We had discovered yet another false-fronted village center on a coastal route, only this time monolithic burl stump formations and other scattered forest remnants surrounded this particular old general store-turned wood gallery.

A man large enough to handle these behemoths of wood greeted us, eyes sparkling with a quiet resolve of purpose. My enthusiasm for the amazing wood formations around us became readily apparent, and our host, Phil Clausen, responded with a tour of his studio and patient answers to my barrage of questions about his menagerie of forest artifacts.

A fireplace adorned the main front room of the old store, where Phil had crafted a striking wood artifact into a structure to frame the bricks. Sometimes, an ancient, gnarled myrtle or maple, or even cedar, will grow a scar tissue-induced, wrinkly border around a decayed hollow at the tree trunk's base. This formation from a massive tree trunk is what Phil had incorporated into the design of his fireplace by cutting a cross section away from the hollow and showcasing the single piece with its wrinkled edge while effectively shrouding the fireplace opening.

I had used many similar formations to good effect and pegged the term "regal rustic" as an appropriate description of the wrinkled exterior tree sections that grow over dead wood and hollows. *Live edge* is the common term to describe wood slices that retain the tree's natural skin along the sides of the cut slab. Both natural forms can be polished into an appealing luster, and worked well with rustic furniture creations like Phil's.

Large whimsical creations of found wood were Phil's hallmark style, up to giant dining tables wrought from one slice of burled wood. Sizable mushroom-shaped lamps were a Clausen signature creation, and many of his pieces utilized the raw material of myrtlewood.

It was a pleasure to meet Phil Clausen and discover his old general store showroom of remarkable wood creations. A fourth generation of the same river valley area of the Coquille River, he knew the land, forest, and rivers harboring colossal tree remnants, and he pursued them for his large-scale wood art. Upon mentioning my interest in the rare tiger-stripe form of myrtlewood, Phil procured a chunk blazing with the figure, sawn off from a larger project, and put in my hands.

On these inquisitive missions to the coast, I made it a point to explore other myrtlewood shops and their impressive works in wood. The Coos Bay area is easily a mother lode of myrtlewood, both in the resources of her forests and the activities involving the wood.

This is where I first crossed paths with Bayview Manufacturing Company and their Myrtlewood Chalet outlet in its original location. The Chalet in North Bend and the House of Myrtlewood of Coos Bay stacked up as the major competing players in the industry and I visited both, but my experience at the Chalet would prove to be life changing. As I walked up the steps and paused at the gift shop door, wood workers brought out three freshly created myrtlewood elephants, finely detailed and sized to 12" by 5" thick. Astonished, I reveled in the realism and workmanship apparent in the light-cream colored hardwood of these particular elephant carvings.

That was all I saw in the shop—and all I wanted to see. I went directly to the sales office, talked the talk of many questions, and was quickly shrugged off by the sales rep of owner B. Roger Clark. Yet, four years later, in 1979, he and Clark paid me a visit, pulling up to my modest home in a big black Cadillac. They then proceeded to seriously analyze my early artworks in myrtlewood, including an elephant mother and calf wall hanging, and within a month of that encounter I began carving the same elephants, those that had so inspired me years earlier, at the new Bayview Myrtlewood factory.

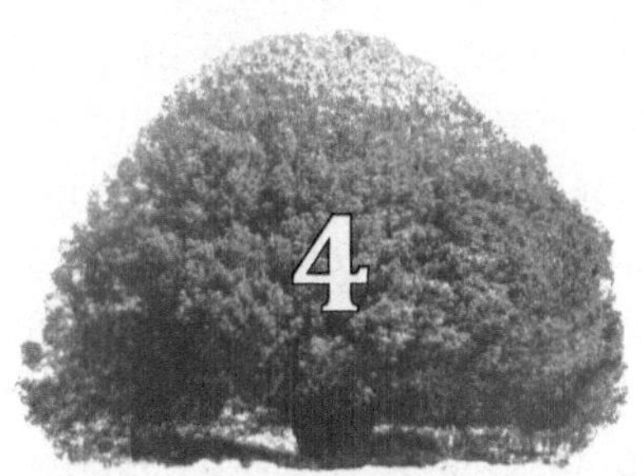

4

The Greatest Myrtlewood Show on Earth!

B. Roger Clark started every morning early at Mom's Kitchen, a small café conveniently located across the street from his Myrtlewood Chalet establishment. For many years he simply walked across the street from his myrtlewood shop until a change disrupted this comfortable routine. He still partook of breakfast and small talk at Mom's, but afterward climbed into his pickup truck and headed north on coastal Highway 101, lighting a big cigar as he went. As the stream of smoke vented from his chawed-on stogie, a stream of plans, problems, and potential solutions poured through his mind. It was a full five miles to his new destination, four of which were tempered by rolling sand dunes bordered with evergreens: miles of white, soothing sand hills with a tidewater estuary at their base that all ran parallel to 101.

It was at the base of these dunes and where the estuary came to an end that Roger expanded his myrtlewood empire and where he had the world's largest myrtlewood factory built. Fronting on Highway 101, the mill bordered the very northern-most extension of the physical Coos Bay. He now owned and operated a 40,000-square foot sheet metal factory built on 15 acres, manned by up to 30 employees, and up to seven myrtlewood shop outlets from one end of the state to the other. Mr. Clark had a lot to keep track of.

Work ethics and protocols at Bayview Manufacturing Company were similar to any wood production plant. Personnel were expected to remain at a work station doing their assignments, except when transporting materials or attending to other requirements. Production was heavily enforced, with many, many different products consistently on the factory floor.

Most emphasis was placed on the profitable turned trays and bowls, with men tackling the roughout and turnings and women sanding them. Many flatware items required band sawing and machine sanding, and a separate spray booth room provided finishing with lacquers. A full-sized sawmill with a substantial log yard occupied a separate building from the main factory and provided a more than adequate supply of raw materials.

With his large-scale myrtlewood factory, B. Roger Clark provided services on many levels. The vast inventory of raw stock was immense enough to welcome other smaller shops into the supply fold, with occasional amusing results in the action between certain buyers and the sales dynamics at work.

On one occasion, the owner/operator of a mytlewood shop to the south, Bob Tuck, was on the floor at Bayview to purchase some lumber. B. Roger Clark was overseeing his selections from a cart of ½" boards when suddenly the buyer began shuffling through the cart, knocking boards asunder as he grabbed at the prettiest grained boards for his limited purchase. Roger scrambled back, trying to retain the best colored wood for his own factory use. An emphatic tug o' war developed right before my very eyes, as these two shop owners literally fought over the best choices of myrtlewood!

As evidenced by this tug o' war, management at Bayview was well aware of the seductive allure of this fine hardwood of beautiful grain colors and patterns. New hirees felt an extra zeal, triggered by the opportunity of working with this raw material, which translated into favorable production on the factory floor. Eventually, however, the assembly line work of noise and sawdust and repetitive production of the wood items could wear down even an enthusiastic wood worker.

Most employees among the core group of skilled and longer term staff had pet myrtle projects, and many impressive works were accomplished on the side. For example, Curtis, the spray booth operator, crafted superb model fishing boats. Yet other workers resigned themselves to the production routine only for the paycheck, with no more interest in the raw materials then if they'd been working in a popsicle-stick factory.

I, on the other hand, considered myself in it for the long haul, buoyed by my goals and dreams, and intent on learning and fine tuning the skills of creating wild life sculptures in this expressive wood. I had dreamed long, and had finally joined the ranks of this myrtlewood factory, billed as the largest in the world, because that was where they had a carving department.

I have to admit, there were times my idealistic nature received an attitude adjustment from John, the foreman, who reproached me once with a curt and comical, "What do you think this is, some kind of a myrtlewood boys' club?" John, a muscular and take-charge kind of guy, who perfectly fit the role of a hardwood plant foreman, continued to lecture that this was a "for-profit business, not a have fun-with your-wood-project hobby center."

While at one work station, I paused at a rather aggressive machine nearby that turned iron hard blocks of myrtlewood into various products. Seeing my distraction, John exclaimed, "Welcome to the wobble right factory!" The Sheetrock wall behind the work station was embedded with numerous errant blocks that had flown off the spindles of the maverick machine at an obvious high rate of speed and force. Some blocks had even marred the ceiling a good 20' above the cement floor. I suppose they were left where they'd landed as a warning for the benefit of other operators, or possibly because nobody had ever bothered to wrench them out of the Sheetrock.

During a dreary cycle of gray skies and endless winter rain came an assignment that proved this Bayview work force was definitely not a "myrtlewood boys' club." Whether management considered me loyal and dedicated enough for a dirty job, or just tough-guy foolish enough for it, I do not know, but on this day I was the employee targeted to solve an unpleasant problem.

An emergency was unfolding at the factory with flood waters engulfing the parking lot and threatening the factory building. Management simply put the challenge before me to solve this dilemma and had me marched out to the edge of the flood disaster with no way out "as mandated by the boss." I was game. In truth, I actually welcomed the outdoor diversion. That is, until John ordered me to strip down to my underwear. Endless rain might be a normal pattern of midwinter weather on the Oregon coast, but as I stripped down, the rain could just as well have been spears of ice pelting my skin.

It seems that some of Mother Nature's other wood carvers had been busily chewing through small trees and branches and packing them into a solid dam at the opening of a large culvert. The industrious work of the beavers, combined with the constant rain and high tides of the adjoining slough, had effectively created a small lake between the factory building and the high berm running parallel to it that supported Highway 101. And the waters were rising.

The plugged culvert ran under the highway, and that was my destination. With a long pole in hand, stripped to my skivvies, I waded into this mini-lake almost up to my waist, dodging drift debris and willow tangles. The swirls of currents were enough to test my balance, while I braced against the numbing winter water. Finally, closing in on the clogged-up tunnel, I began poking and prodding at the giant bottle stopper with my pole. By leveraging out one mass of sticks at a time, I began to make some progress, all the while slipping against the constant fluxing that increased as the dam loosened.

And then, with a last plunge of the pole, victory! The barricade broke open enough for the water pressure to do the rest. I quickly backed away as the currents rampaged into the culvert and the water level began to recede.

Trudging back to the edge of the parking lot, I slowly regained my composure—and my jeans. John had kept watch on my progress, encouraging me on when needed and acting as a makeshift life guard. In a gesture of empathy, he let me go to my home nearby to change before returning to my work station in the factory.

I could embellish this story if the work order awaiting me back at the factory involved the carving of beavers. But, although there was a 6" tall standing beaver in the carving department lineup and I had produced dozens of them, it didn't happen to be the work of that day. Plenty of jokes about carved beavers in the pipe line ensued following my drenching, however, and they inevitably showed up in my work assignments later on.

The carving department was located in an approximately 40' x 60' sectioned off area complete with a dozen work stations. This included four ribbon sanders, a flat sander, a small band saw, a drill press, a handheld electric-grinder and work table, a couple of flex sanders (used for critical finishing steps), and various supporting tools and supplies. Other operations not related to carving also occurred here, such as the fine sanding of trays. Shortly after I first walked onto the floor as a new hire, I had set my anchor, and this area quickly became familiar territory.

Besides the equipment, the busy carving center also had its own lineup of quirky characters that I was destined to join. David managed the stylized and smoothed style of figurines, mostly working with a ribbon sander for shaping and band sawing out his designs at the communal band saw. David led management on for days with procrastination and a monkey act on a high platform that he constructed for his work station. This consisted of his sander, a tall stool, and bright lights, all elevated on stacked pallets that gave him an out-of-reach, psychological edge over the prodding of his overseers.

After enough taunting, though, David always came through, working long and hard like a highly skilled maniac, doing a week's worth of assignments in a day or two. He could play these games with the bosses, aggravating them beyond measure, because he had hard-to-replace skills and, in the end, always filled the orders.

David excelled with the fully sanded abstract figurines, such as the smooth-formed seagulls mounted on a stylized base, and was knowledgeable and innovative about the workings of myrtlewood. With David's help, and that of an artist named Ken, I learned all the sawing, sanding, roughing out, and burr grinding steps and skills to attain the proper shapes and proportions of animals and birds. This proved to be relatively straightforward work, but the rounding of heads and bodies by sanding had its challenges, mostly in maintaining uniform sizes.

Pleasing, consistent proportions were attained by repetitious practice, of which there was no shortage when on-the-job production demanded carvings in large numbers. For example, one morning at the start of the shift, a large bin of over 300 small bird-shaped cutouts from the band saw was delivered to my work station. I commenced to shape and finish-sand one after another for the duration of the week. When they left my hands, they moved to the spray booth for a finish of clear lacquer, and then on to sales distribution.

A flex sander apparatus, which is a key trade secret, provides a crucial tooling step for contours of carved bodies and heads. This action completely rounds and smoothes the pieces, as was done with the aforementioned birds, and is the last critical step before the spraying of lacquer finish. For the extra hard wood of myrtle, tougher than usual sandpaper strips are hand cut and fit into the cartridges that load into the circular flex sander body. The commercial sand paper inserts ready-made for the machine simply cannot do a satisfactory job on a wood of such density.

Ken was an accomplished artist of oil paintings, and did the finer work in the carving department on a two days per-week basis. As my main tutor in the work of carving myrtlewood animals, Ken guided me through the step-by-step processes, producing the more lifelike figures that took extra time and finesse. I was happy to work with him on these pieces and grateful for the wealth of knowledge and skills that I attained.

At this stage of my apprenticeship, I particularly liked the praying hands mini-sculptures we created for the Christmas and Easter seasons, and took them on as a special challenge. Executing such eloquent, detailed work needed to be masterfully accomplished. In my mind, while working on the hands folded in prayer with their aura of piety, they became a symbolic icon of hope on my chosen path to become an accomplished myrtlewood carver. My adamant desire to do the best work that I could possibly muster held strong until, after carving them in numbers, I had succeeded in producing quality renditions over and over again.

Many years later, after I had left the firm, I learned that, though the praying hands were a popular item during the holidays, they'd been dropped from Bayview's line of carvings. Sadly, it had proved to be too difficult to produce an acceptable replica.

One particularly elusive step in the carving process took the steady hand of an artist to accomplish the desired results. This step consisted of cutting lines in the wood using a handheld power grinder mounted with a diamond shaped cutting burr. This tool with its special bit did the same job as a handheld veiner knife, as both tools cut a "V" shaped groove as it passes through the wood, resulting in details such as the fine line of a figure's mouth.

While working on a run of salmon, which required many details provided by the diamond burr, I was stymied by the challenge of cutting straight and true lines in sometimes distorted wood grain. Eventually, Ken became impatient with my efforts and, with a dismissive look, exclaimed to the floor manager, "I'll do all the line cuts that need to be done on Terry's carvings."

Fortunately for me, the floor boss overruled his "request." "I want Terry to learn all the steps to complete the carvings on his own," John said, and that was that. I was relieved with the verdict and, ultimately, with plenty of repetitious practice, I mastered the skill of laying down straight and even lines, as if drawing with a pencil, but using the grinder with the diamond burr instead. This skill continued to be an essential asset for all my future works and helped seal my status as an artist.

John had hired me at the beginning of my stint at Bayview and throughout his tenure remained my advocate for achieving the skills needed for animal carving. I qualified as an asset to the production of carvings and many other factory operations requiring a thorough knowledge of myrtlewood, and John opened the doors to much of that knowledge.

One of the production line philosophies in the carving department was to achieve a fully sanded, completely smooth surface throughout. That was the ideal: a minimum of tool marks except a few veiner lines for details. The more simplistic, stylized carvings were basically mass produced knick-knacks, and the more sanding surfaces the better. Sanding brought them quickly to a finished stage that was acceptable in the hands of the buying public, and production time remained minimal.

"This isn't even carving, it's just sanding," Ken complained when working those carvings. "Nothing artistic about it." He was in charge of the animals that needed more detail and required some tool marks left on the completed piece. He gave me the impression that the more textural variations resulting from the work, and less sanding, the more artistic the work became.

I saw different possibilities for these carvings by striving for more tool marks instead of fewer, texture in place of smoothness. I was savvy enough to follow grain directions correctly with tool strokes to avoid the rough and torn grain that would be unacceptable in a fine carving.

Thus, I developed my own style by adding personal touches to the production carvings. This proved particularly effective with the more sophisticated carvings such as the large elephants. Tooling was effective for muscular legs of mammals, feathered effects for birds, and anything else that benefited from extra texture, such as the bumpy, barnacled snout of a humpback whale. In the future I would carry over this style into the pieces I designed, such as the aforementioned humpback whale that became successful in my own line of myrtlewood sculptures.

As my skills became more polished and producing carvings became routine, I worked closely with Ken on major challenges, like the large elephants. He was always pleasant, once commenting, "When you get into this rhythm with a carving, it's like playing the violin." Bringing a piece to a polished and satisfactory finish was like the curtain call. Many times I heard him mention working "that good wood," as only someone immersed in creative work with the material would understand. Some things can't be taught. It's about following your instincts and going with the flow. Even though Ken only worked part time, when he left the firm I was saddened to see him go, and carried on with the realistic animals on my own.

Our textured, realistic carvings produced at Bayview included small and large elephants, standing bears, striding bears, ponies, beavers, ducks, cats, salmon, small squirrels, frogs, sea lions, sperm whales, bulls, horse head book ends, and praying hands. Smooth-sanded, abstract, non-detailed carvings produced consisted of small birds, medium birds, Madonna, religious fish, owl heads, deer, and sea gulls.

I managed to conquer one seemingly far away dream after another in this pursuit of my career. First, just to be carving animals for a living had seemed like a fantasy, and here I was doing just that. Another vision I sought that seemed like an unattainable dream was matching grain patterns with the patterns of animals, particularly the tiger. This I accomplished by producing a limited series of nine tigers, carved solely from the fantastic tiger-stripe grain running wild through a rare and select myrtle log.

A run of sophisticated carvings like these tigers began in the saw mill, and could only be achieved when the rare striped log showed up in the log yard. I arranged this special run by working on Saturdays and being paid per piece, for a once-only limited edition. With my lofty wildlife carving goals utilizing an exotic wood, these tigers crowned an epic achievement of my early career.

Tiger-stripe is just that, a dusky tan wood with a multitude of jet black streaks running through it. If you look at the cross section of the log's end, you can see black dots peppering the heartwood. When boards are cut parallel to the log, horizontal stripes appear throughout except in the ring of sapwood. There are various theories about the source that triggers the markings, and most such pigments, but not all, are found bordering decayed centers of the tree.

For any artist there is always the frustration with labor time versus product saleability, and this formula had to be profitable, especially at a factory like Bayview. Such a great variety of detailed, desktop size animal carvings produced in large numbers is dependent on one magical duplicating machine. Known as a spindle carver, this vital piece of equipment roughs out 18 animal shapes at once by following a previously carved pattern. Band-sawn blocks are set into spindles that tighten, all in a consecutive lineup in a framework. Interconnected router heads spin above the blocks on arms controlled by the operator, who runs a stylus over the model. Wherever the stylus moves, the router heads follow, cutting away material from all the blocks simultaneously, until the shape of the animal pattern is complete.

These blocks were generally sawn out from green myrtle, as the cutting knives worked through the material easier than on dry wood. Also, the more material removed, the easier the drying process. Once the animals came out of the dry kiln, the creative work of finishing them began.

One exception to the kiln drying step was the large elephant, which measured 5" thick, 10" high, and 12" in length. This was a premium carving, and only small numbers were produced. Because of the large areas of end grain on the pieces, where cracks tend to form, extra care was required. Elephants were roughed out and sealed with lacquer on the end grain, then buried under wood chips in a cool location for up to a year to slowly air dry. This heavy, closed grain hardwood had to be coaxed along in many ways to ensure satisfactory results.

The shortcut provided by the "Carver Craft" duplicating machine, as Roger would call it, was especially effective for the long- legged-animals that have lots of material to remove between all the legs. This is a particularly daunting task for a sculptor, and where the stupendous labor-saving machine proved its worth. The main creative step of the process entailed hand-carving out the model, much like the clay mold made by the sculptor for a series of bronze replicas.

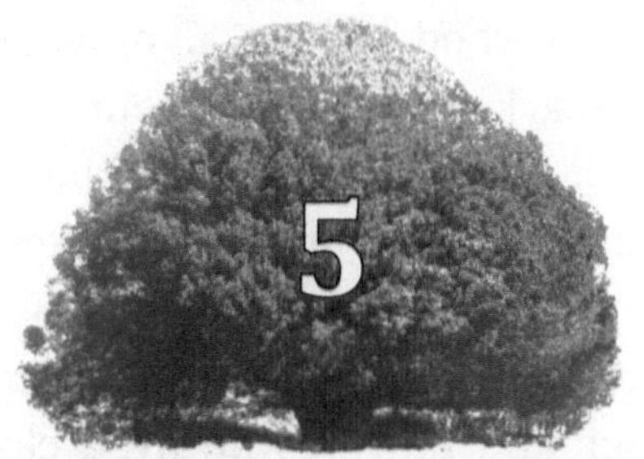

5

Spectacles of Tree Wood

All the time that the myrtlewood factory was churning out its products, a critical aspect of the business was quietly playing out in a gutted-out old house swept with sand dunes a few hundred yards away. Lee, a tall and crisply featured guy said to be of Native American heritage, worked here at his own pace, creating magnificent burl wood coffee tables that, along with burl clocks, were a popular mainstay of the coastal myrtlewood industry. Apparently, this shell of a house suited him fine, with plenty of weatherproof areas where he could work with the messy concoctions of fiberglass resin necessary for the final coatings of the table tops.

Sand dune roads converged here, with a few modest residences scattered about, all in close proximity to the Bayview myrtlewood mill. A former old folk's home that was now a pile of ruins was wedged against the hills of sand, with a feeble-looking sign proclaiming it to be The Solarium as it leaned over on its way to oblivion. Thick clumps of pines and firs bordered the dunes and effectively isolated one building from another.

Lee's humble facility served as a stopover for seasoned wood suppliers, a regular mecca for myrtlewood insiders, complete with coffee and tall tales. I was eagerly drawn to this inner circle of wood experts, all of whom were cohorts of my boss, Mr. Clark. During lunch hours at the factory and short stints after work, I'd gobble up their idle talk about outrageous burl formations and their strategies of acquiring and utilizing the finest myrtlewood.

One afternoon, Bob, a log broker and hauler, Lee, the table maker, and Edwin, who lived close by, were all engaged in the latest myrtlewood talk. As I came around the corner of the building, crows could be heard in neighboring tree tops as if they were announcing my presence while competing with the tempo of the conversations.

"I'd give my left nut to find one of them onion burls!" Edwin emphatically proclaimed, as the others nodded in agreement. Edwin had big ears that stuck out from the side of his head, and when he became animated over these legendary burls, his eyes widened as if they were trying to outdo his ears.

"What's an onion burl?" I blurted out. I had to ask. They looked at me as if I were an upstart probing for state secrets, but Edwin loved to talk wood searches. "It's a tuber-like growth. Can be a large, round burl forming from the roots." Somehow, all three men seemed to know that this rarity of all rarities had to harbor the most spectacular myrtle grain possible.

"They can be huge, and all growing underground," Bob the log expert added, "and very rare." Of course, being underground would make this the most elusive burl of all, I thought. Bob was usually all business, supplying logs and making connections for quality material. He and B. Roger

Clark occasionally scouted out the best quality logs for the mill together.

As a logger knowing the forested landscape, Bob touted the Rogue River area as harboring the best myrtlewood selections in terms of coloration. Always alert for extraordinary color contrasts that are guaranteed to aid in product sales, Roger made a priority of acquiring these Rogue River specimens. He even paid extra to Menasha Corporation, a timber operating company, to set aside truckloads of only the finest myrtlewood logs found on their lands up river from Gold Beach, a coastal town at the mouth of the Rogue.

Besides aiding Roger, Bob was generous with advice and connections for other serious myrtlewood purveyors and helped me obtain wood cutting permits years later for the carving business that still remained in my future. One of the truths I later discovered was that highly valued myrtlewood with extra coloration can be found throughout its range. The Coos, Coquille, and even the Chetco river drainages have provided me with some of the richest myrtlewood one could ever hope to procure.

In all my years of salvaging myrtlewood stumps and logs in forests, rivers, bays, and ocean beaches, only once have I come across an underground growth that could qualify as the mystery onion burl. It still lies where it was found, too inaccessible and labor-intensive to harvest by hand. I did expose enough of the tuber-like growth to verify its form, likely the swelled growth of a large, individual root.

One of Edwin's tools of the trade was an oversized, military-style boom truck that couldn't be missed when announcing its presence close by. The rusty red relic, an old Dodge power wagon, had a substantial winch line running up and through the boom, making it an effective crane for all of Edwin's wood-gathering needs. Oversized airplane tires ballooned out from its sides, making it look as if it could float across the many ponds dotting the dunes, and assure easy access to any driftwood-strewn beaches within many sand road miles.

Both he and Bob supplied large burl formations to cut for Lee's tables. Edwin procured the weathered driftwood giants, and Bob accessed burls from logging sites in the coastal mountains. They had found and shared many spectacular burled wood formations, many myrtle logs streaked with vivid colorations. Yet there they were, still intent on finding the ultimate holy grail of myrtlewood, those underground onion burls, wherever they might be. The excitement was as much about the chase as it was about the treasure.

Lee was content to work the rough-cut pieces brought to his shop without going anywhere, whether up mountain slopes or down wandering sand roads. Once in a great while, an oversized, burled log showed up at the Bayview sawmill and choice slices were set aside for Lee to work into tables. He often sanded the table slabs on a 12' long stroke sander stationed in the myrtlewood factory, after which his finished work was destined for Roger's showrooms. In fact, Lee was supplying the Myrtlewood Chalet with tables from this humble dunes locale even before the nearby factory was built.

Slices are cut for table tops across large tree stumps and boles studded with burl outcroppings, which reveals marbled beauty of grain. Swirls and curls around bird's eyes are found throughout, which makes these burled slices so spectacular. Also, a cross cut such as this would have unexpected bark pockets and erratic shapes around the natural live edges.

Once the pieces are sanded smooth, Lee went to work with resins and some creative touches. All of the defects usually found in these natural cross sections were filled in with layers of clear plastic resin. The larger bark pockets and decayed centers were adorned with tiny sea shells, small dried starfish and sea horses, and dried sea grass, all set in sand until the look of a tide pool emerges in one part of the table top. Layers of liquid plastic seals the oceanic tide pool scene in place, and three full coats are poured over the entire table. The finished result is a clear, glass-like, hard finish that is a window into the myriad patterns of wood grain beautifully integrated with the look and feel of the ocean.

Lee mounted his table tops on other natural wood formations selected for their rustic character and stability in supporting the top. Most of the time the organic-looking table base was also coated in resin to match the top. Like a fireworks display, the swirling fantastical myrtlewood figure burst forth, raised into view by the base and amplified by the resin glass coating.

The finished products were exceedingly popular with their sense of the coastal area. Besides the resin-coated clocks and tables, optional natural finishes of oil or lacquers were also utilized, resulting in a more subtle and serene myrtlewood coffee table. Those finishes generally required a defect-free surface of wood crafted along the lines of fine furniture.

This was an iconic approach to creating myrtle burl coffee tables that reflected the flavor and look of the Oregon Coast, and helped visitors identify myrtlewood art and products with the coastal highway atmosphere. Enamored by all the artistic applications that revealed themselves in the myrtlewood region, I actively sought them out, eager to create some version of art combining rustic wood with the creative use of resin, although I shied away from resin-coating an entire piece.

For these new inspirations I went no farther from Lee's table shop than a few hundred yards around the sand dunes. There, a low-profile building constructed from machine-smoothed logs nestled and served as the new Myrtlewood Chalet gift shop. Only a half mile from Bayview's myrtle-wood operation, it set back against the dunes, yet still benefited from open access to Highway 101.

At this stop, I marveled at Lee's finished tables and reviewed products coming from the nearby factory that lined the shelves. Besides being gratified by the animal carvings coming from my own hands that were in the mix, I soaked up the artistic expressions of many other contrib-uting artists. Colored pencil-and-ink drawings on rustic myrtlewood panels depicting western-flavored wildlife and Native Americans was a specialty of artist Alix Mosiuer and an ongoing favorite of the Myrtlewood Chalet.

Bayview's sawmill activity resulted in slices off the outside of logs containing a perimeter of natural live edges that gave a unique character to the boards. Cut 1" thick and stacked in separate units, these were known as "rustic boards," and had many creative uses from clock blanks and cribbage boards, to paintings with artistic flairs utilizing the wood forms and grain. I was assigned to bandsawing out and edge sanding these forms quite often, until it became something of a specialty. Although basic and routine work, I appreciated the experience as it carried over to working up bases for sculptures and other uses in my artworks of later years.

During one work session, B. Roger Clark was overseeing my work as I stacked and sorted a cart of rustic boards. I was eye-to-eye with Roger when a perfectly formed small image of a wild goose appeared in a spalted board. As the flying goose image magically appeared on the board, I stopped and marveled at it, and glanced at Roger.

Had he seen it? I wanted to pull the board out, to save the image. But because he was the owner and top boss, I was too intimidated to draw attention to the uncanny image or pull the board out, and so continued with the discipline of my assignment, burying it forever. In hindsight, I think Roger might have appreciated a pause in the work to at least admire the remarkable natural image, but the strict protocol on the factory floor left little room for distractions or diversions from the work assignments and prevented that from happening.

A ribbed black material forms the inside of many hollow myrtle logs and around the base of half hollow stumps. When this material appears in the rustic board slices, the wood can be used for astounding artistic effects. Artist Roberta Schmidt, whose artworks were a regular addition to the Myrtlewood Chalet's offerings, was particularly skilled at painting ocean waves and seagull scenes around these appendages and deformities, blending them in as craggy cliffs and unusual shorelines of natural wood.

I was drawn to the rugged textures and rich colors of sanded grain that appeared alongside these forms, and compelled to create some version of art combining these rustic pieces with carvings. After appreciating Lee's tide pool scenes arranged in the resin coated burl tables, also on the showroom floor, the use of plastic resin again came to mind. Later, after some brainstorming thoughts had gelled,

I envisioned ocean scenes with the addition of carved birds and sea animals.

I began experimenting with resin dyes to create ocean waves and shorelines against the backdrop of the black ribs of texture in the rustic wood. I then perched small carved sea lions of light brown wood on crags and promontories, with occasional whales embedded in the blue resin "water." Mixing white resin dye into the edges of the blue resin produced the effect of whitewater waves. Adding a thin, flat board surface above and behind the textured areas served as the sky, where I set a scattering of carved seagull forms in a gliding posture. A final finish of lacquer completed the attractive, oceanic wall hanging.

Eventually, I expanded these scenes to groups of dolphins leaping above the water, stained orcas, spy-hopping whales with emerging tails, but almost always including a group of sea lions in barking mode on the ledges. These oceanic creations proved to be a popular offering in coastal shops close to home and a sales success from the walls of a local restaurant catering to tourists.

At one point, I focused on carving leaping salmon and placing them above resin water cataracts spilling over rustic ledges. This series found wall space in the Umpqua Valley Arts Association's gallery in Roseburg, Oregon, and none of them returned to my home studio.

With a passion to share my newly invented work with the art world, I directed my efforts to the dockside old town of Newport, Oregon. I had arranged an appointment at the Wood Gallery, a dominating edifice anchored to the historic bay front and a preeminent art gallery of the area.

After the 100-mile drive up the coast, gallery personnel instructed me to wait on the sidewalk. Though the summer heat glaring from the pavement was discomforting, I was willing to wait this one out. Time passed slowly before the owner finally came padding out to meet me on the street. With a commanding posture highlighted by a sharp outfit of matching khaki shorts and shirt, it looked as if he'd just come back from a casual summer safari. Though I had been hopeful at the outset, after a reasonable survey of the work that I had for him in my car, he declined to hang my ocean scenes in his gallery, and gallantly waded back into his busy establishment. I was disappointed, but, as every other artist knows, rejection only fans the flames of creativity, and I vowed not to be deterred.

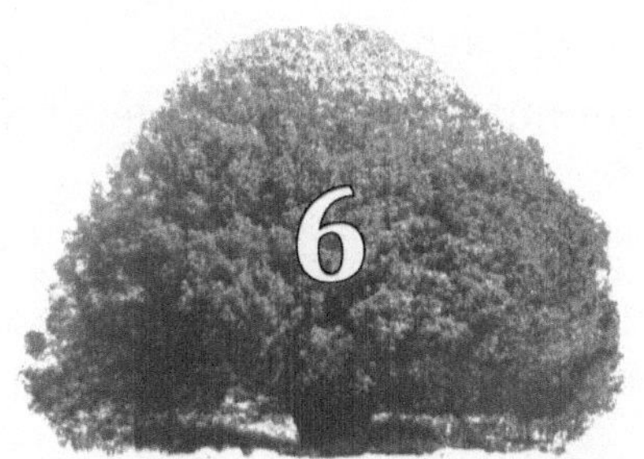

Hardwood Transformations

At Bayview, the log yard and sawmill together were the engine driving the entire myrtlewood factory. This layout consisted of a flat acreage that accumulated decks of logs by deliveries of two to three truck loads at a time, and an adjoining building that housed the sawmill. This building also served as the "green end" operations of breaking down fresh planks into manageable products that were moved on to the factory dry kilns en mass. Many stacks of fresh lumber also went into the kilns to be cut out for a multitude of products down the line.

An ancient and giant relic of a front-end loader deposited logs selected for milling at a big bay door opening close to the head rig. The logs were then bucked into 8-9' lengths with a chainsaw, loaded onto a conveyor belt with a forklift, and advanced to the head rig carriage. The head rig consisted of a double-bladed circular saw powered by an electric motor that easily handled the average log diameter of 20-40", since the main circular blade boasted a diameter of 48". The lower auxiliary blade worked in tandem with the main upper blade, and its 30" diameter helped handle any log up to 4' thick and more when the sawyer rotated the log after each swipe of the blades.

John, the foreman, operated the head rig, cutting a run of planks for the factory once every four to six weeks as the projected cycles of products dictated. Due to this tight-grained hardwood's long drying process, it was essential to cut large amounts of stock well ahead of the time it would be needed.

On rare occasions, Roger also did the cutting for its diversion from his upper office, relishing some of the nuts-and-bolts operations at the source. There was more inspiration in that head rig for Roger because he envisioned what it meant for the future supply of select wood for the factory and sales.

Although my position was technically in the carving department, many times I was also recruited to assist John in the loading of logs and off-bearing the heavy planks as he cut them. Time spent in the "green end" also engaged me in cutting out raw stock for the carving department.

I enjoyed the intrigue of this work, the mysteries found inside these gnarled and twisted forest remnants that unfolded as we worked. There was always a selection of bumpy, burl-encrusted behemoths, specimens banded in multiple colors or peppered with tiger-stripe and, on rare occasions, boles black as ebony. This initial process was significant in that we were at the source of supplying the entire factory production.

Myrtle trees retain a significant amount of moisture, and their mass can be 70% water. Although a large tree trunk might lie on the forest floor for decades, when cut through, it will be as wet inside as the day it sprouted. Some of these fallen trees steadily rot away into forest humus, while the heartwood of others remains intact for many years. It all depends on the particular resin content and chemical structure of the individual trees, for the heartwood generally remains long after the sapwood and bark disappear.

One such moisture-laden specimen, a fresh-cut tree bound for the circular saw, was literally a deep green and dripping to the extent that I have never seen before or since. The log was extra heavy, at least 30" in diameter, and the fresh cross-cut log end revealed a deep, juicy green color with black bands circling throughout. This denizen of the rain forest is a good example of the unexpected and spectacular material that can be revealed from within a random myrtle tree.

Let's take a look inside this resplendent bole and follow it through the processes that lead to so many admirable works in wood.

Much of the stock from this fresh log was typically earmarked for the factory bowls and trays. However, I set aside a generous selection of choice green-and-black banded planks destined for carving stock. Since the 4" x 10" duck carving was currently much in demand, I used their pattern to band saw out these ducks and loaded the cutouts onto the carving-shaper machine. Operating this machine and shaping numerous pieces at a time for a week resulted in dozens of wet roughouts that were loaded into the dry kilns. I also worked up salmon and other carving selections to best utilize this prized material.

After six weeks in the kilns, all that juicy green dried out and transformed as if by magic into a deep, rich yellow.

The black bands intensified even more, creating a brilliant contrast of black and yellow throughout the carvings. The challenge with wood that is this dense and moisture-laden is its inevitable warping and shrinkage as it dries. Many of the roughed-out bowls cut from this tree were a total loss, especially since six weeks is really too fast a drying cycle for this extra-dense wood.

However, the carvings were unscathed since they could still be finish-carved into slightly smaller renditions and altered, if necessary. Warping that caused a duck head to twist or turn, for example, could still be carved with even more character added to the piece. In the months following, an amazing series of finished ducks and salmon emerged from the carving department after that one significant tree was laid to rest and transformed into life anew.

Although I spent many hours cutting out blocks and operating the spindle carver, I did not have the privilege of carving wildlife full time, especially in my early apprentice years. With two full-time and one half-time carvers, I had other work delegated to me off and on. Many processes in the factory were of interest to me, and I was eager to observe and learn everything I could about the applications of this incredible hardwood, and John encouraged a wide range of training practices.

The majority of this side work piqued my curiosity and passed the hours agreeably. In one instance, the Rainbow Factory put in special orders for extra high quality myrtle-wood boards. An eye for the wood was necessary for these orders, since they required only the ultimate colorations and character of grain. Selections made for the Rainbow Factory orders included ebony black, tiger-stripe, heavily spalted, intense burling with extra colorations, and other outstanding features. Identifying and sorting out top grade wood of great beauty was a privilege, and I felt honored to be chosen for the task. Dried units of 1" thick boards were run through the large and highly efficient 48" wide belt sander to fulfill the Rainbow requests.

"It's all steak and no hamburger for this order," John told me. After a moment's thought, he reiterated "No, not just steak. This one's all fillet mignon!" While the boss ran the boards through this giant machine, I selected out and stacked only the most incredible colors and figure for the Rainbow owner. A unit of boards measured 8' plus in length, with a 4' width and height. Less than 10% of an average unit qualified for the Rainbow Factory, and the owner paid extra for that top-end, high-grade material, three or four times more than the usual rate. This selection process demonstrates the variety of myrtle grain, and the rarity of the finest colorations.

But some of the side work assigned me was nothing more than brutal labor. Besides my typical carving work, hours of grueling assembly line work landed on my plate, such as sanding small discs, one after another, day after day, until a bin full of thousands were the only merits of my labor. After some of these mind-numbing episodes, I found myself walking it off on a nearby ocean beach, where all that sand seemed like endless fine grains of sawdust coming back to haunt me.

I was here for the carvings, and I was hungry for more animal figures, not multitudes of jam jar lids (those tortuous discs). I approached Roger with my dilemma, and requested a piece work arrangement whereby I could work on numbers of extra carvings outside of factory hours. Roger was open to the idea, given it would add more lines of carvings for his shops. We agreed on prices and subjects, which started out with small squirrels and a line of frogs that would be an addition to the carving department's inventory.

In this way, I got my fix of extra carvings to work on and earned extra money at the same time. Most of this piece work was accomplished on my back porch with an electric grinder and drill after shaping the pieces with the factory's spindle carver on Saturdays, my day off. Roger must have been amused that my solution to mind-numbing work was to add on more work!

Roger made his final request to move forward with the deal, telling me I'd need a business name so that he could make checks out to me. With this encouragement coming from the man in the driver's seat, I made a major step forward to establishing my own business. I returned the next day with my new business name: Pacific Carvings.

In a morale-building move, management decided to make company uniform jackets available on an optional basis. Most employees snubbed the yellowish-beige attire, but I felt intrigued by the offering. I had lots of pride in my work and the Greatest Myrtlewood Show on Earth, and discovered that green patches with a myrtle tree in the center were available in the gift shop. I bought one, my dear wife Carlin sewed it on the breast pocket of the generic jacket, and I began wearing it on the factory floor. Lo and behold, before long I wasn't the only one wearing the company-issued jackets with the green emblem of myrtle-wood pride added on.

Seeing that my enthusiasm lasted well past the burnout stage, Roger put more stock in my work and allegiance. By this time, Rick the Foreman had replaced John the Foreman, and when Rick directed me to a rather plain log for carving stock, Roger intervened and instructed me to bypass the foreman and select the carving stock myself. He knew that the resulting carvings would benefit from my grain selections and that the new floor boss lacked experience with the intricacies of myrtlewood.

Shortly thereafter, near the end of my employment at Bayview, and in a great twist of irony, David the carver took the reins as foreman. The promotion could only be termed an ultimate case of poetic justice from his days of playing the management. When I merged full time with my own business of Pacific Carvings and said good bye, I left the company and all my friends like David on good terms.

The last run of carvings I produced for Bayview was a delightful collection of ponies. Spotting a rare tree of solid black heartwood highlighted by a small ring of white sapwood that bounced out of the log yard, I immediately earmarked it for carvings. This particular chemical composition of myrtle is by far the rarest form, a tree wood that is solid black like ebony. Of all the hundreds of logs that I have laid eyes on, only three or four have been of this configuration, leading to the conclusion that only a small percentage of trees grow this way.

I roughed out at least 18 jet-black ponies from this exceptional material, which also carves crisper and cleaner than the average carving stock. When cutting out from the pattern, I even managed to arrange the slender band of creamy white sapwood to give a few ponies white socks.

These testimonials provide a cross-sectional view of specialized operations in a myrtlewood factory. My four years employed in a myrtlewood factory may seem exhausting to you, the reader, but this was a necessary foundation of my career. The learning and application of these skills proved essential for the accomplishments that were to follow and the art work still to come.

At the one and only Bayview company picnic, at least during my tenure, a well-restored antique Model A Ford sedan chugged up to the parking lot curb. Eyes bright and seeking new passengers, the driver puffed on a big cigar as his charges disembarked. "We rode clear to the moon," quipped one. "What!" I asked, perplexed. "Moon Creek, just up the road," came the reply.

Yes, Moon Creek flowed into the North Fork Coquille River a mile upstream from Laverne Park, a forested camp-ground hugging the banks of the river and the location of our picnic. Not to keep B. Roger Clark waiting on his joy ride offerings, I piled my family into the antique machine for the next ride. Without traversing the moon, we clattered along for a fulfilling tour of the park.

Most of the Bayview picnickers were in the spring and summer of their lives. Young families, newly married lovers, a few old hands, all joined in for the carefree gaiety that prevailed over the event. They were all good, hard-working people, some "just passing through," and some part of the corps of dedicated workers that kept the myrtlewood factory humming year after year.

As the potluck and softball games unfolded, the gnarled old growth myrtles lining the park stood witness as they had for centuries. Prolific residents throughout the park, they could not miss the irony of a gathering of people from a factory that gobbled up their brethren. But their brethren were felled regardless, and the factory gave new life to their cherished wood rather than burning in funeral pyres at far-away logging sites.

So, I like to think these myrtles relaxed with this celebratory mix of humans and tucked away the dark shadows of a dreadful event they had witnessed in Laverne Park a few years earlier. And surely they could not know what some of the old and decayed sentinels among them would fall victim to in the future.

ERA OF OPULENCE

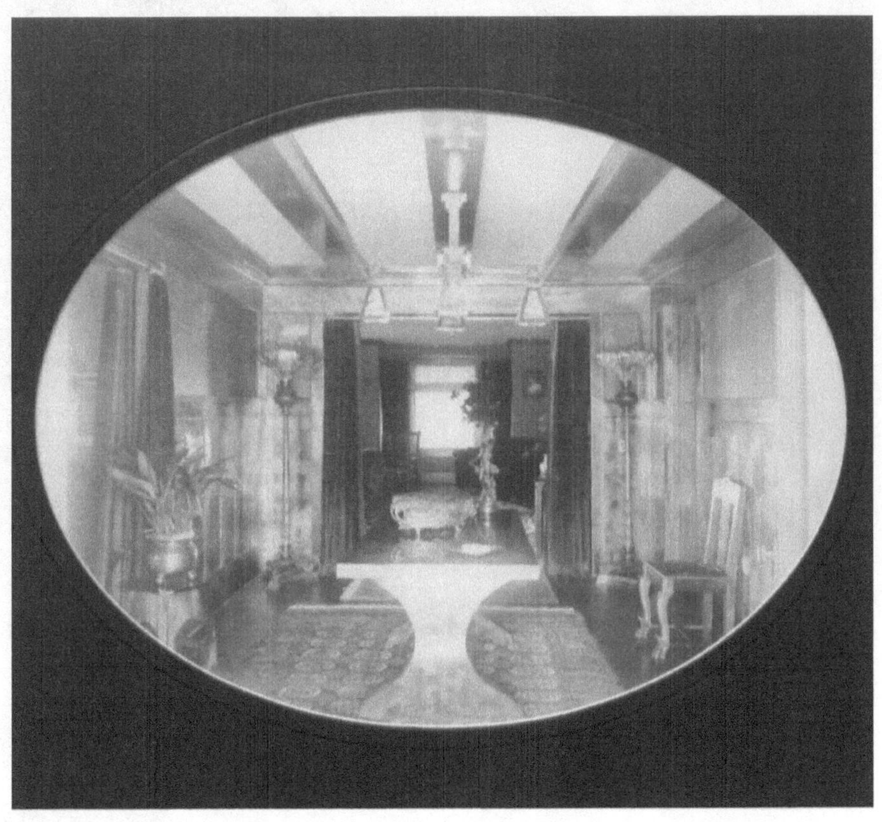

Entry hall into the Shore Acres mansion overlooking the ocean southwest of Coos Bay, Oregon, built by Louis Simpson in 1906. Myrtlewood table in center, walls paneled in myrtlewood.
Courtesy of Coos History Museum, 003.9.13.

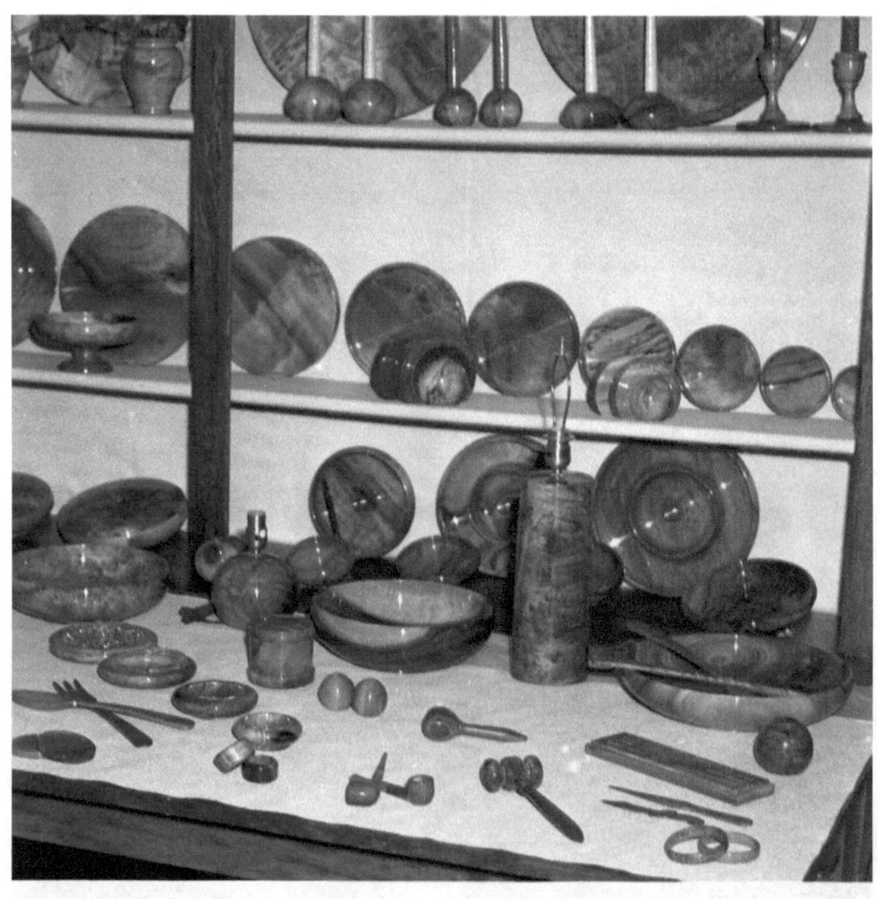

Myrtlewood turnings, the most prolific usage of the wood. Upper shelf, large trays, candle stick holders; middle shelf, stair step sizes of plates; bottom counter, assorted bowls, nut bowls, lamps, salad tongs, salt-pepper shakers, napkin rings, smoking pipes, gavel, bracelets, letter openers, cribbage board, and a paper weight.

Courtesy of Coos History Museum, 991.N125 f.

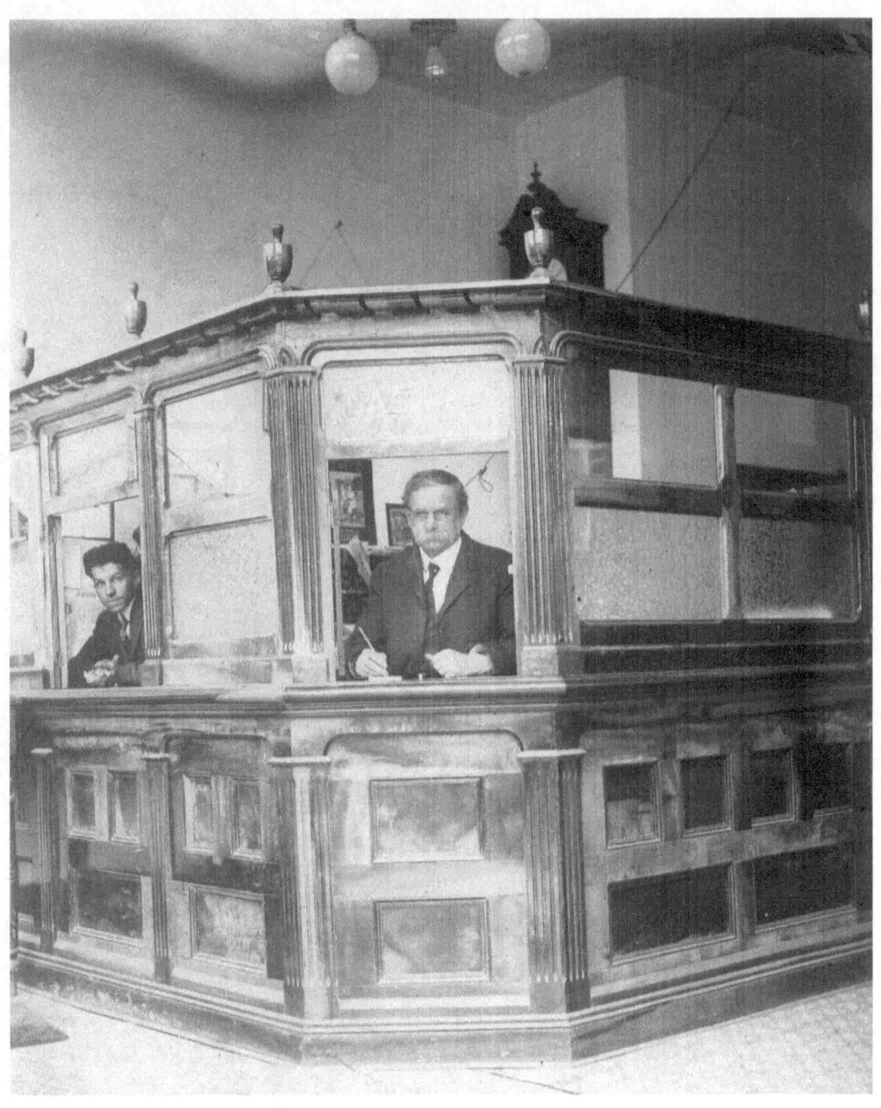

Bankers who mean business at the helm of a beautifully garnished myrtlewood teller's counter, Bank of Myrtle Point. Perhaps the stern looks are due to a 1913 incident, when a robber cut a hole in the office floor above the bank, dropped into the vault area, blew open the strongbox with nitroglycerin, and liberated $10,000.

Courtesy of Coos History Museum, 967.137 t.

On the far right we can see the eyes of pride, eyes of dedication to perfecting the craft. Leaning on the left, a no-nonsense bull-dog forging ahead into the everyday demands, perhaps as an overseer. Center, a crofter that knows how to master his craft, humbled by the marbled wood grain held between his hands. All gone now, swept away along with the wood chips and sawdust piling up on the floor from their labor. Oerding Manufacturing Company, early 1920s, Coquille, Oregon.
Courtesy of Loreena Oerding.

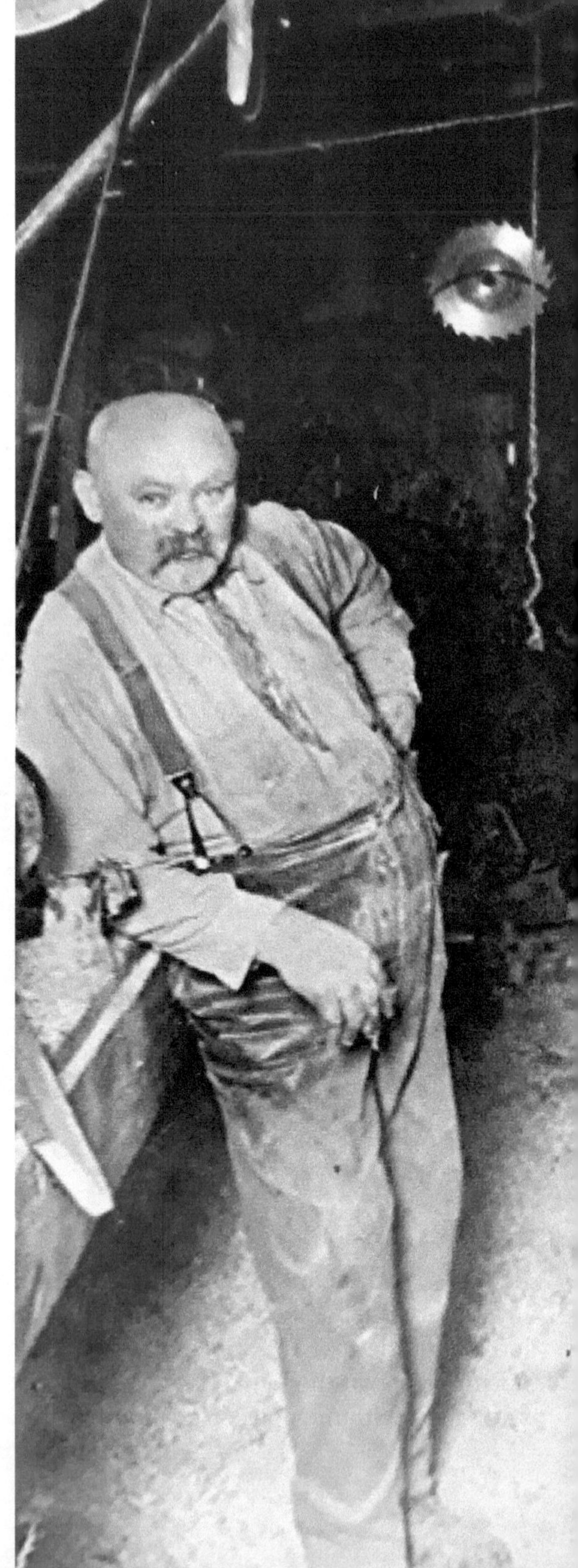

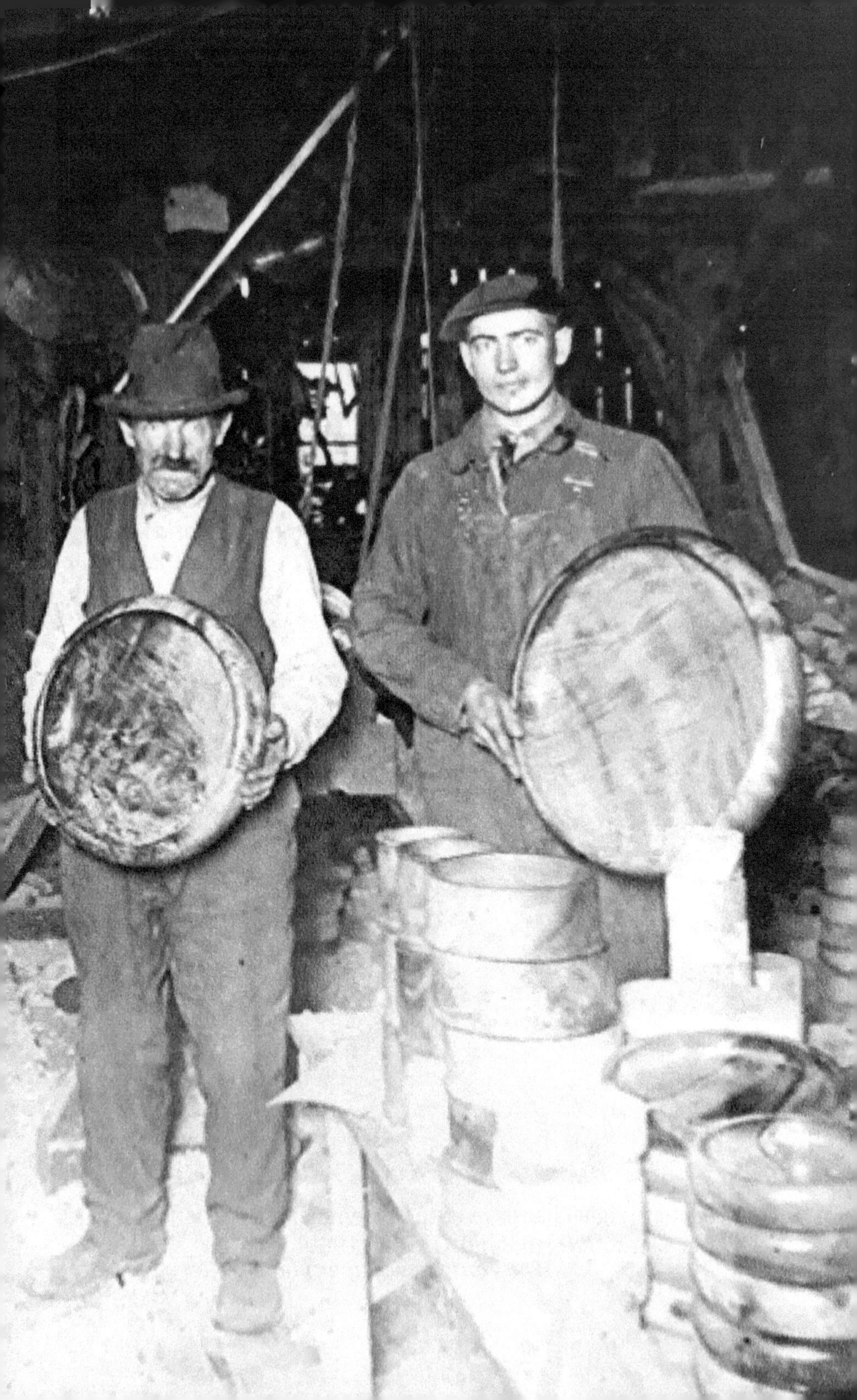

IN THE NEWS

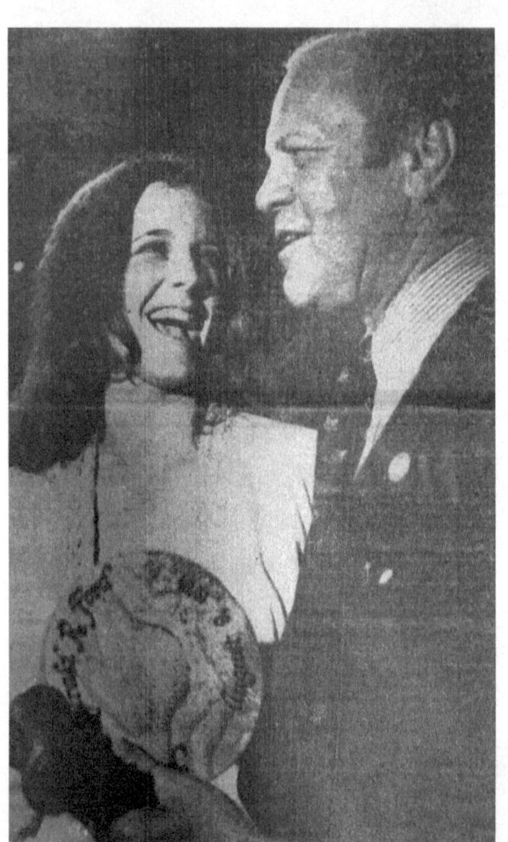

Tricia Streeter presents President Gerald Ford with a myrtlewood plaque and gavel from the House of Myrtlewood during a GOP fundraiser in 1974.

*Courtesy of Coos Bay's
The World newspaper,
UPI Telephoto.*

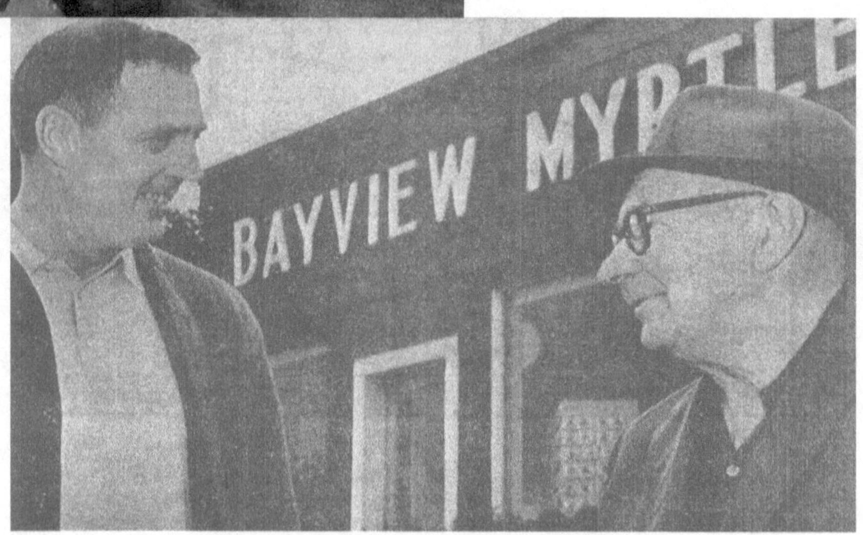

John Reiher (right) hands over the Bayview Myrtlewood keys to B. Roger Clark in North Bend, Oregon, 1969.
*The World newspaper photo by Jerry Stonebraker,
Courtesy of Judi Larson.*

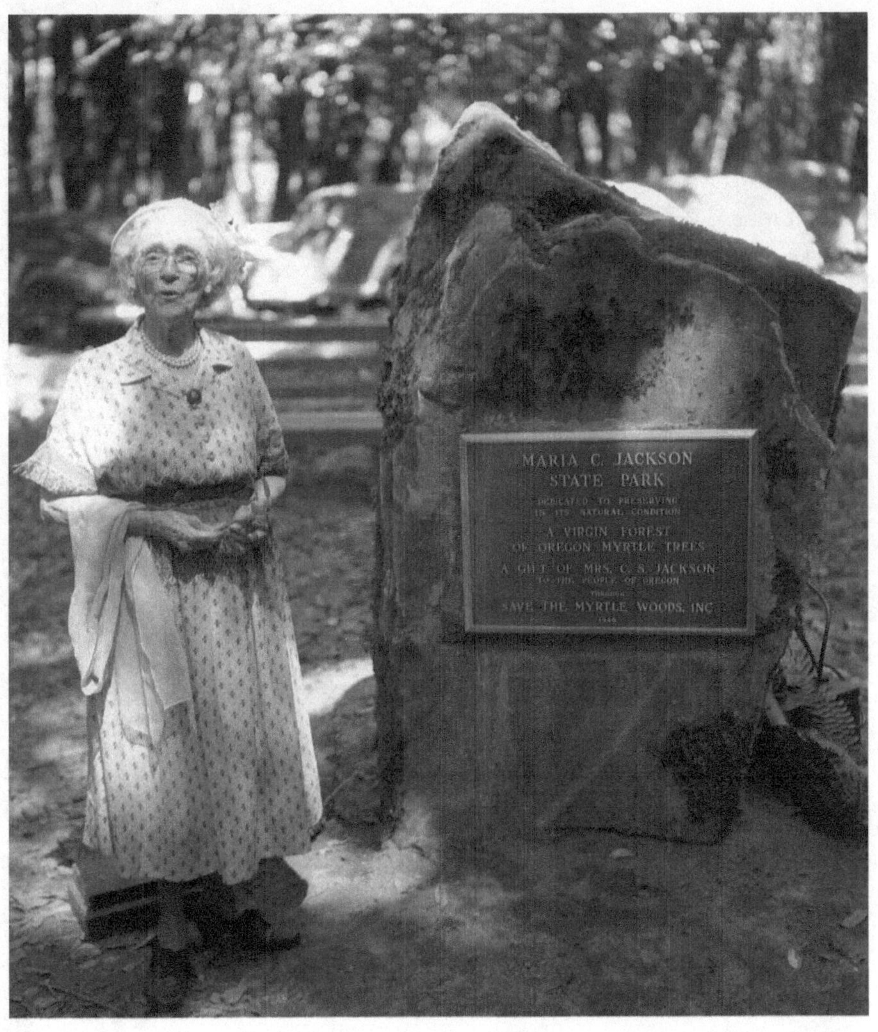

At the christening ceremony of Maria C. Jackson State Park in 1946, Maria C. Jackson poses alongside the stone monument and bronze plaque designating the park in her name on behalf of Save the Myrtle Woods, Inc. The site remains a wilderness park of myrtlewood trees near the hamlet of Sitkum, Oregon.

Courtesy of Coos History Museum, 995.1.10945.

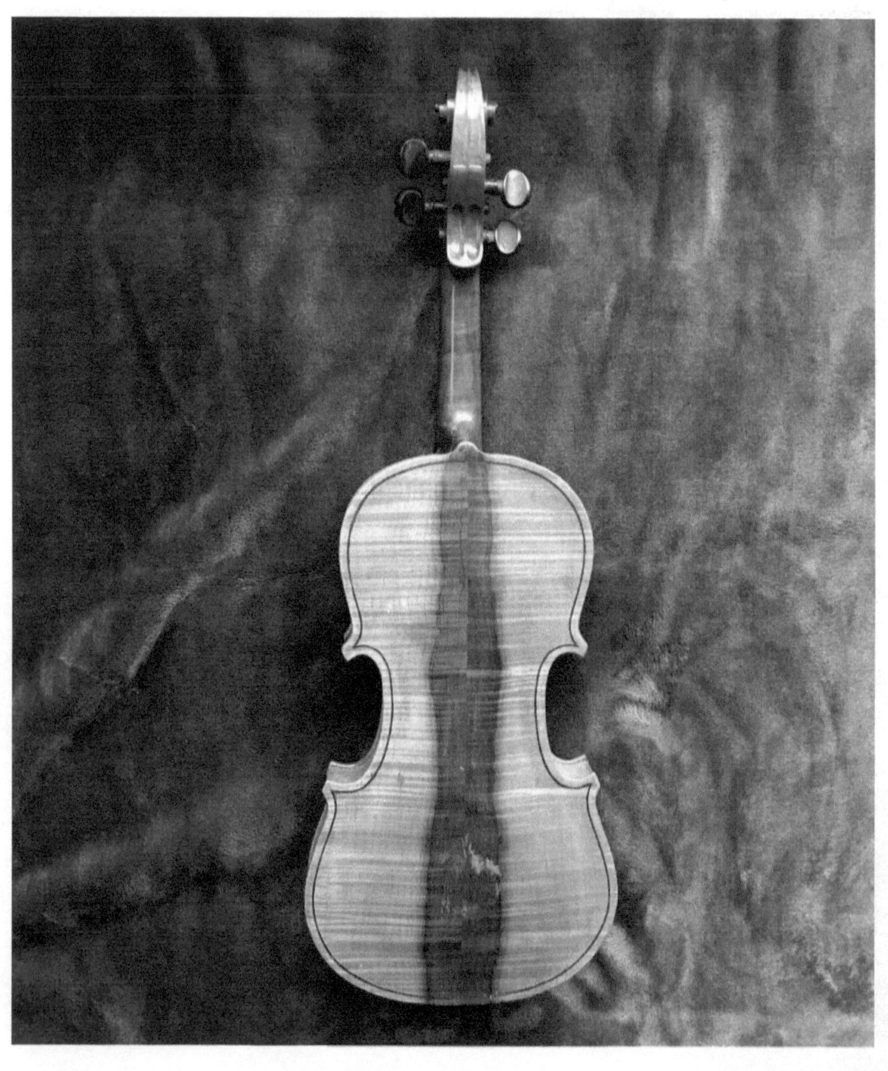

Violin made from curly grain (fiddle back) myrtlewood with a spruce sounding board, crafted by William Marshall Humbert in the 1920s, Coos Bay, Oregon.

Courtesy of Penny Humbert.

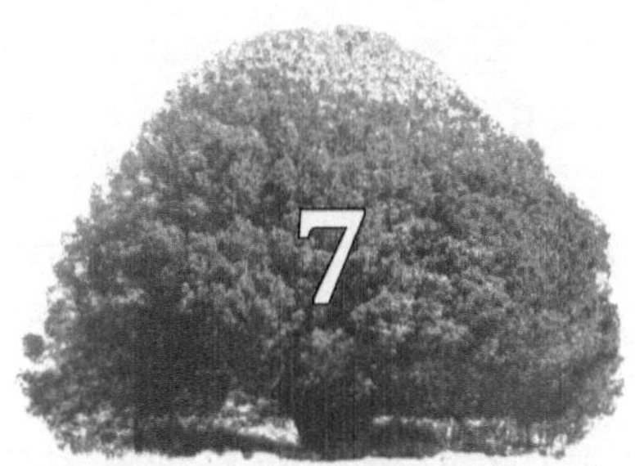

How To Make a Grown Man Cry

It was now 1960, and a new phenomenon sprang upon the cities of Oregon and elsewhere. We saw the opening of the Lloyd Center in Portland and the Pony Village in North Bend, the first indoor shopping malls built in the state. Pony Slough, which ran by the North Bend mall site as it emptied into Coos Bay, became the namesake of the new shopping center. Within a year, my mother Juanita, always on top of the latest trends, drove my sister and me over from the Umpqua Valley to visit this new marvel close at hand. At that time, I had sprouted up with 10 or 11 years under my belt.

From the '60s on, indoor shopping malls evolved into thriving community centers, and Pony Village Mall, the largest one on the Oregon Coast, was no exception. From this wellspring of activity came a flourish of people with varied interests, crossing paths and swapping stories. Besides the army of employees operating shops and restaurants, notorious locals, who "lived" at the mall, were there almost every day from opening to closing.

By the early 1980s this hub of local commerce offered an epicenter of local wood interests, including B. Roger Clark's Myrtlewood Chalet outlet, and, specifically, a shop named Nature's Wooden Image. This establishment owed its success to Bill Leslie, a personable born-salesman, who rounded up an offering of exceptional wood art and products, much of which came from the local region.

Bill Leslie showed an unabated enthusiasm for local myrtlewood work and the unique fauna of our sea coast. One of his visions was to expand his shop with a special Whale Chamber to contain the best of local whale-themed art, complete with recordings of whale songs filling the atmosphere like an aquatic sound room.

Bill saw that I shared much of the same interest and gave me a leg up with my own career pursuits. His uncle, Al Hashberger, owner of Beaudette Myrtlewood, produced a line of myrtlewood products called perfumers, small vase-like wood turnings hollowed in the top-center so a vial of perfume with a cap slips in. Many perfumers even advertised the myrtle tree's own aromatic oil as the scent inside.

Hashberger developed expert techniques in applying lacquer finishes that best enhanced the grain and did justice to the delicate turnings with their petite character and exclusive usages. The secrets of a fine finish like his would be indispensable for my business of Pacific Carvings. Bill introduced me to Hashberger and helped arrange a workshop session where I could learn more about these fine finishing techniques. To this day I still use the same equipment and finishes that I learned from that session.

As I came and went delivering my carvings to Nature's Wooden Image, Bill flagged me down one afternoon to chat about another myrtlewood craftsman who brought items into his shop. "He really likes your work and wants to meet you," suggested Bill, and passed on something about the craftsman's myrtlewood sources. Hunger for workable myrtlewood loomed large in the early days before I acquired the means to cut my own wood, and I quickly agreed to meet up with him.

When I returned for the rendezvous after a soon-to-follow workday, a man with a round face framed by dark wisps of hair and amplified by large glass lenses greeted me with a peering owl look. As I shook hands with Lloyd Bechtel, the older woodworker's optimistic enthusiasm shone through and his easy drawl proclaimed an admiration for my carvings.

Wood art of all sorts surrounded us in Bill's establishment, and I complimented the workmanship of my new acquaintance's cribbage boards that he was delivering for the store shelves. After a bit of sparring about myrtlewood supplies, we both agreed that black and tiger-stripe versions of the wood were the rarest and most sought-after forms. "I have a couple of gunstock blanks loaded with those colors that I will give you, if you come up to my place," he ventured.

What? Over the years I'd become accustomed to wood enthusiasts talking the talk, but not really walking the walk, and I'd learned to be patient and courteous with drawn-out conversations. My first reaction was skepticism at such a generous offer, but his sincerity and likability put me at ease. Lloyd did not seem to be one of those types, and all I had to lose was a little time.

With Lloyd's directions, I found myself cruising up the Coos River until I veered up a tributary road that led farther into the coastal foothills. The moon played hide-and-seek with the clouds as I went, until it finally chased them away to illuminate a long, sloping driveway. Lloyd came out from the house at the end of the drive to greet me with the same enthusiasm that I had experienced earlier at the shopping mall.

After I spent some time admiring his inventory of crafted myrtlewood cribbage boards and other novelties, I noticed some beautiful burl-grain wall clocks. I blurted out my immediate pressing question. "Where and how did you manage to acquire such spectacular rustic wood grains like these?"

"Well, you have to know these mountains, but the source of these clocks is really hidden in plain sight almost everywhere out in this logging country," he teased. "Perhaps I can show you someday."

From his back porch inventory, Lloyd led me to an outbuilding of miscellaneous uses, including storage. As he held a flashlight, I found myself crawling and squirming under the building, groping among stacks of myrtlewood. Judging from the dust and cobwebs, the special stash of planks scattered before me had been gelling for a long time.

"Those pieces, right there!" he pointed with his flashlight. "Drag those pieces out." After I pulled myself and the myrtle treasures out from under the structure, we both marveled at the charcoal colorations showing through the well-aged gunstock blanks.

"These are for you," he said. "I'd like to see some nice animal carvings come out of them." I thanked Lloyd profusely, promising a carving or two from the exquisite material just for him.

While I chased the endless needs of a young and growing family, Lloyd, a grandfather and a generation older then my 30-something years at the time, purchased a portable wood mizer sawmill. This band saw mill sat upon a trailer frame, giving Lloyd the versatility of hauling the saw unit to forested logging sites where he enjoyed scouting out the finest of myrtlewood logs. After sawing the select material, he also enjoyed sharing the bounty with other woodworker friends.

Late one summer evening, the phone rang, and I picked up the receiver to hear a punctuated, "You better come see this!" spilling out from the other end of the line. It was Lloyd, who gave me directions to some undeveloped Coos County park lands on the North Fork Coquille River.

The county had a fleeting project for a shooting range here, and the local National Guard was recruited for developing the wild site. The land to be cleared was a wide flat prairie that ran up against escalating hills of thick fir forests. From two opposing directions the angled ridge lines gradually descended, pinching off the valley floor until they met where the winding river had cut its path. At this apex where the river canyon left the abrupt slopes, a verdant prairie crowded the mountain wall with a maze of creeks that chased the river and turned swamp-like in the wet months of the year.

This ideal terrain saturated with moisture incubated and enriched the thick myrtle stands; it was likely that some concentrations of colorful figure would appear in the wood grain of these trees. The occasional passerby would never know what sylvan mysteries were present in the imposing myrtle giants that dominated the marshy fringes of this prairie. I was eager to delve into some of the enigmas from their growth.

I found Lloyd with his portable mill parked amongst a scattering of myrtle logs from a giant tree he had felled. Front-end loaders, trucks, and other equipment, along with a crew of National Guardsmen, were moving earth and brush around for the project. "They wanted this tree out of the way, so I took care of it for them," Lloyd explained. By helping with the clearing of land, he had access to all the myrtlewood that he wanted by moving the trees and logs out of their way. Ultimately, the county abandoned the shooting range project, and all the verdant parkland of Rock Prairie reverted back to nature, sparking the slow renewal of its groves. In the meantime, there was wood to salvage.

I looked around at the impenetrable brush and thick trees towering overhead, all firmly anchored in the rich black soil of the marshland. The crews had cleared an extensive opening on the edge of this temperate jungle of tangled myrtle and maple trees. "Come on, this is what I called you about," Lloyd beckoned, and we strode over to the edge of the clearing to a hodge-podge of brush and limbs shoved up against the verdant wildwood.

There lay the remnants of an ancient tree, unrecognizable as the tree it had been. Branches, bark, and all the sapwood had long ago decayed away, leaving only a 35' long core of tree trunk measuring 20" plus in diameter. This relic could easily have been settling into the forest floor for centuries.

"I saved this one from the burn pile where it was heading," Lloyd beamed. My jaw dropped as I noticed where the blade of a Cat had scraped a spot clean on the log. It gleamed like a freshly polished pair of shiny black shoes. "Enough to make a grown man cry!" he chimed, using his favorite phrase whenever fantastic, otherworldly myrtlewood appeared before him.

Without hesitation, I offered whatever it required for cutting and utilizing this profound relic of the forest. "I want every sliver of this wood," I proclaimed, "all the outside rounded rinds, every knot and remnant, everything!"

Lloyd looked at me quizzically, knowing my modest means, and thought about all the black sawdust that would pile up under his sawmill. "You want all the sawdust glued back together into boards as well?" and I laughed with him.

His price for cutting the planks to my specs fit my monetary standing in life, and I'm pretty sure he generously adjusted it that way. Of course he was due any boards of his choosing for himself. At the time, I did not even have a pickup truck with which to haul the wood, just an old Toyota hatchback that served as a family car and a wood hauler as needed, and one modest-sized chainsaw. In spite of these shortcomings in my young life, sheer desire and ambition kept raw material for carvings within my reach.

The wood of a black myrtle tree is much denser and heavier than average myrtlewood, with excessive warping and shrinking occurring as the stubborn moisture slowly respires after it is cut into planks. In its own wet environment of the temperate rain forest, high moisture content is the norm: again, even centuries after the tree has fallen, it remains as wet as the day it was born.

In between the cutting of this black log, I scouted around the myrtle swamp for other exclusive grains. Sure enough, we rounded up three or four other trees that were rife with tiger striping. The magical minerals mixed in the black earth of this prairie, along with the constant water saturation, contributed to the pallet of Mother Nature that had infused these myrtles with an extraordinary concentrate of colorful figure. With help from others, it became apparent that rare forms of myrtlewood supreme for carvings were falling into my lap. It may sound like an incredulous claim, but the fact is, my 32nd birthday fell in the middle of this bountiful wood harvesting episode.

Lloyd manned the sawmill while I did the heavy lifting as we turned the black forest artifact into a treasure trove of exotic material. Much of his motive in cutting myrtlewood was in the joy of sharing this wealth of wood native to our region. That, and revealing the astounding grain found in choice logs gave him satisfaction beyond the monetary values. Meanwhile, visions of sea lions and whales, seals and dolphins, swam through my mind as we laid eyes on the fresh cut shades of ebony. Lloyd's proclamation echoed in my head, and it was "enough to make a grown man cry."

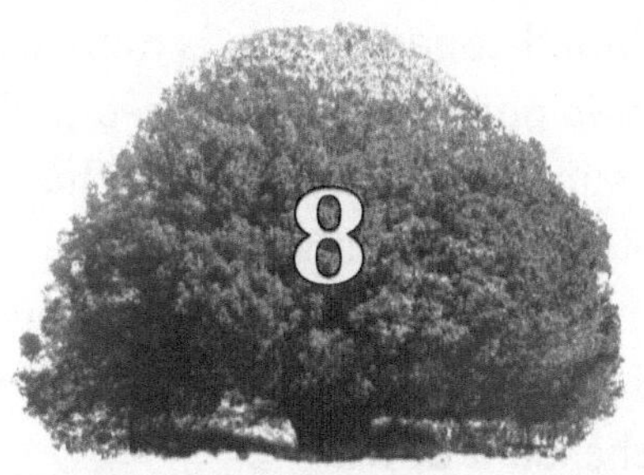

8

JEST UP THE ROAD

I furthered my dreams of carving wildlife by slowly acquiring the necessary equipment for producing carvings in my own shop, an endeavor that had begun on my back porch and graduated to a garden shed and then on to a double-wide mobile home that had seen better days.

Once I began working myrtlewood full time for Pacific Carvings, my own business, it became imperative that I attain self-sufficiency with wood supplies. Cutting my own resources also made sense because time and labor involved with one sizable log provided months of carving stock. It may not be surprising that creating myrtlewood products of any kind is extremely labor-intensive, and conscientious craftsmanship adds even more hours of extra care for the final creations.

Because of its wide-ranging virtues, success with myrtlewood is achieved by accessing the wood with the finest grain colorations, something accomplished by salvage-logging and careful selection of materials. As a rule of thumb, only one out of 10 trees host the extreme figure for which myrtle is famous, although sometimes the desirable trees dominate in one specific location. The older, mature trees usually have better odds of rich colors; otherwise, plainer, blond-toned myrtle is more common.

Up until this point, I had bartered and bought planks from various suppliers and wood enthusiasts, some like Lloyd Bechtel who operated portable sawmills. That changed when a newspaper ad appeared for a portable chainsaw mill available in the nearby town of Florence. I immediately chased it down.

It was a simple but sturdy unit of steel, parked in the shop the owner had built with timbers cut by this same mini-mill. I was impressed, paid the price, and loaded my jeep pickup. The 20' main steel beam stretched across the top of the cab and down past the tailgate, but the entire unit was easily accommodated, essential for my future plans of transporting it to myrtlewood sources. As I drove away, I was elated with this acquisition and the wealth of resources it could provide.

After 40 miles of easy highway and no incidences with the cumbersome load, I began the last winding rural miles homeward. Halfway through the hilly curves around the Coos Bay, taken at a slow and careful pace, a car began tailing me. Night had fallen, and its close headlights punctuated the driver's impatience. I considered pulling over to let him by, but no, I thought, it was just a few more curves to the mile long straight stretch of roadway where he could easily pass.

As we came onto the long, flat route, the driver wasted no time accelerating around as I paused to let him by. To my dismay, as he made the move, his left front tire dropped off the pavement and began vibrating erratically, threatening any steering control of the vehicle.

This long straight is built up as a dike road parallel to a slough waterway on one side and a sunken pasture lying below the other. The limited shoulder edge is just beyond the fog line, with sheer drop offs of 10'-15' on either side of the road.

The black sedan racing around my jeep was tempting fate on the pasture side of this causeway. Suddenly, to my horror, the car went completely out of control, careening over the bank, flipping end-over-end, taking out a telephone pole until it rolled back to its upright position facing the opposite direction in the middle of the pasture.

I hit the emergency flashers, backed up, jumped out, and, with limited shoulder room, left my jeep in its lane. It was then I recognized the black car sitting in the middle of the pasture as that of a friend living in the nearby vicinity of country homes. Our daughters played together and were school classmates; he and I played in weekly basketball games, many times commuting into the town gym together.

"Dennis!" I hollered over the embankment, "Are you all right?" I was stopped from rushing down to his vehicle by strands of heavy, live electric lines brought down to waist level by the clipped-off power poles. I hesitated, knowing I could leap over the wires and roll down the bank, but Dennis's response stopped me.

"I think I'm okay, don't try and come down here," Dennis called out shakily. Perhaps he could see the power lines in front of me, since the driver's door now faced the road. We both knew that the electric field of high voltage lines could suck you onto the wire like the pull of a magnet on metal.

"Are you alone, is anyone else in the car?" I shouted urgently. One of my biggest fears was for his wife and daughters.

"Just me," Dennis assured me as he struggled out of the wreckage. "I'm going to try and get up there."

I warned him to watch out for the electric lines.

Dennis, a short and wiry guy, climbed over a barb wire fence, shinnied his way up the steep bank, and managed to wriggle his way under the dangerous power lines. He appeared alright, but as I surveyed more of the damage, he began shivering from the trauma and said he could use a blanket. We were both aware of the risks that shock can bring.

"Let me take you home," I volunteered, and escorted him to the jeep. After three miles at a more hurried pace, I delivered him to his door and family, minus the pizza left splattered all over the inside of his car that he had been attempting to bring home for dinner. After making sure he was okay and explaining the incident to his wife, I hurried back to the accident scene.

When the power pole snapped off, it had torn off a supporting pole from across the road, which was now dangling by a guy wire across both lanes. My immediate concern was to flag traffic around the wreckage, as only one lane could be carefully negotiated by slowly driving under the wire and around the dangling, busted pole.

Arriving back at the scene, I saw that a sheriff had arrived with lights flashing and was parked near the entanglement. After giving him a witness account of the unfortunate accident, I backtracked from the scene. Hitting the flashers again, I stopped about a quarter of a mile from the site, jumped out, and prepared to wave down any traffic approaching the snarled roadway from "upstream."

It was getting late on this country road, which thankfully resulted in a dearth of activity. Things seemed under control with the sheriff guiding any traffic through the maze, when suddenly a vehicle approached me at a high rate of speed. Frantically, I waved at the small pickup that not only veered around me, but completely ignored my warnings as it sped up even faster.

Incredulous, I thought, *He's not going to slow down!* Going at least 65, the pickup also ignored the flashing blue-and-red of the patrol car, and raced on down the straight stretch directly toward the obstacles as if this were a 1/4-mile drag race, or, more appropriately, a destruction derby.

Sure enough, *"Wham, kabam, crash!"* The guy wires wrapped around the light pickup's windshield, shattering the glass, and jerked the broken pole onto the vehicle. The sheriff and a handful of bystanders scrambled for their lives as the small truck slammed through the dangling wire and pole, dragging the whole mess on down the causeway before the guy wires finally pulled it to a stop.

After this incident, I decidedly had had enough. No one had been hit by this whirling dervish, and I was not particularly interested in knowing more about the crazies inside the vehicle. Besides, the sheriff would surely take care of them. I drove up to have a brief, closer look at the results of this latest crash, then turned around to deliver my chain saw mill to its new location without any more diversions.

Throughout all of this unforeseen back-and-forth activity in my jeep, I had barely kept track of that 20'-long steel beam jutting out from the top of the cab and dangling behind the tailgate with a red flag attached. Fortunately, all was well with the load, and I had my new prize assembled and operational within a week.

Intent on seeking out my own raw materials, I attempted to sidestep the norm with the maverick approach of utilizing the immense amount of wasted myrtlewood as much as possible. The acquisition of this portable chainsaw mill put me in a great position to recover some of this forest material to supply my Pacific Carvings business. Utilizing some myrtles for a second chance would only make a small dent in an immense timber landscape, but I felt virtuous giving the trees a new life as cherished carvings.

Slash burns are a necessary clean up after a mountainside is clear-cut for Doug fir, but there is always a substantial number of trees, logs, and uprooted stumps left scattered about a landing site and nearby hillsides. Lesser-valued hardwoods are especially prone to abandonment, and a pool of wealth in my eyes. With permits and permission from timber land owners, I gained in raw materials. Along with the right thing to do, this approach proved effective on a number of fronts, and only needed to support a modest level of production.

I had to go no farther than a few miles up the road from the forest land that we called home and the Pacific Carvings workshop that I had established there to access downed myrtle trees. At the road's end was a mountain of basalt, and where there is basalt, there is usually a quarry to extract this valuable road-building material.

This particular quarry came about as an extension of the pioneer homestead called the Elkhorn Ranch that encompassed hundreds of acres settled with homestead claims by George Gould in 1886. The coastal mountain land had been swept by a great forest fire some years earlier, leaving the landscape dotted with charred snags and wide openings of regrowth ideal for browsing game. The Elkhorn capitalized on these bountiful conditions by smoking venison and other game, packaging jerky, and transporting it 15 miles with pack animals to Allegany and the Coos River system. From there it went by river boat down to the Coos Bay, and on to a San Francisco marketplace via ship.

George Gould's grandson Glae added on 1200 acres that included the aforementioned basalt mountain and developed the Kenstone Rock Quarry in the early 1960s. His son David was running the quarry operations when I inquired about the excess downed myrtle left behind by the expanding rock excavations.

David proved to be a generous and kindly soul who gave me a personal tour of the quarry layout and its various spur roads. Near the entrance to the quarry, he proudly pointed out a landmark fir tree, standing stark and alone, that twisted around into an enormous double tree. Over the cliffs above the main quarry poured a spectacular 100' waterfall, which continued down the valley as Kentuck Creek. From this upper canyon at the end of the valley the mountain stream flowed, on past the deck of my home, on through long estuaries, until it finally emptied into Coos Bay.

From this enlightening tour of timberlands, it was obvious that the roads and hillsides above were rich in myrtle stands. Extra enormous myrtles were in the mix, and David related this anomaly back to the forest fire of 1868 that helped establish the Elkhorn Ranch. "This is one of the few pockets of land that the fire missed," he explained, "so the trees are extra-large along here because they weren't killed back by the fire." With a look of awe, David continued describing this inferno of the forest that had burned unabated from the Umpqua River until it was stopped by the shoreline of Coos Bay.

When we returned to my vehicle, David gave me permission to set up my chainsaw mill and salvage a scattering of myrtles that were downed for a road expansion. Thus began a reliable source of myrtlewood that I continued to procure for modest sums, always salvaging what was already downed by other activities. My acquisitions of myrtlewood from the quarry lands were usually handled by David's brother, Norman.

Norman Gould was an artist, some might say an eccentric one, but an artist engaged in his work none the less. Norm, whose accomplishments ranged from impressionistic landscapes to sprawling nudes worthy of adorning any western bar worth its salt, even experimented with video art early on, while receiving an art degree at Portland State University.

Norm's was a solitary way of life by choice. He lived in a rustic cabin perched on a slope to the side of the quarry cliffs and its waterfall that had once been a summer home for the Gould family. After being raised in the outdoor working traditions of this family, he was just as at home sitting at the controls of a D-8 Cat as he was painting behind the artist's easel.

A massive burl became my first wood-cutting challenge after I finished setting up my chainsaw mill at the quarry location. Norman maneuvered the smooth, round growth attached to its mother tree trunk into position with a tractor. I jacked up the mill and increased its height with blocks to add more clearance needed for the chainsaw bar to manage the oversized burl. The entire operation depended on a single chainsaw to power through the hardwood log and its substantial burl.

In addition to the mill frame, I had purchased a used 090 chainsaw, one of the largest saws offered by the Stihl chainsaw manufacturers at that time. By drilling two holes in the bar, it could be bolted onto the carriage of the mill frame. Operating a hand crank and spool of strong wire pulled the carriage and saw through the wood. My normal milling activity utilized a 48" bar, but in order to handle this sizable burl, I replaced it with a 60" bar.

This particular kind of burl grows smooth and rounded, without the extremities and irregularities found on typical bird's eye formations. This "swirling burl" can extend off the sides of matured tree trunks well above the ground, sometimes bulging off of a main stem high up in a tree. In other situations it forms closer to the ground, but either way it can swell into an enormous wood formation.

When Norman had the short burl-ensconced log in place, we checked the alignment and wedged it into a stable position. Everything had to be just right, for we treated the slicing of this round mass of wood as if it were a gemstone, and approached the unveiling with the fervor of anticipation it deserved.

In a flurry of noise and flying wood chips, round tabletops with marvelous figure fell from the saw like a stack of cards. I made one slice after another from the outside of the globe shape inward, each slab increasing in size until the final piece spread well over 4' across.

These prime rustic furniture pieces were a sight to behold, the fully rounded shapes completely encircled with natural live edges. I caught my breath as the exquisite grain patterns and colors swirled through the exposed surfaces, a true phenomenon of Mother Nature. But they had a long drying process ahead and many hours of craftsmanship before they would ever be transformed into the interior embellishments that were their destiny.

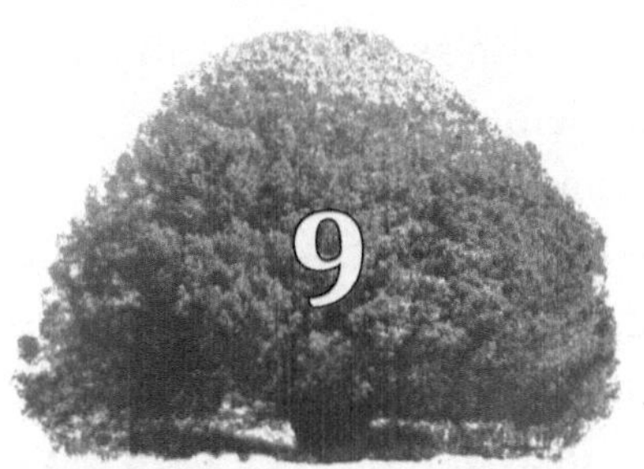

Out Into the World

Engulfed by an aura of optimism, I found myself leaning into the future as the road climbed toward an appointment, to a potential conquest. This cliff-side destination would be the litmus test for evolving into my own business of carving myrtlewood.

Miles of sprawling beach sand fell behind as the rocky headlands took over. Before the sand disappeared, a gray whale rolled in the surf far below, and I slowed down to absorb this rare visual of the large mammal so close to shore. As the whale propelled through the pipeline of breaking waves, its mottled body gleamed through the translucent green tube that formed just behind the white water. It seemed impervious to the water's force as it surged along with lazy strokes of its flukes, bobbing slightly as it stayed in tune with the surf. Soon it disappeared down the coastline, leaving only the waves rolling into the sand that tamed them.

How perfect the natural world seemed, and what a pleasure it was to carve these same marine animals in the grain of myrtlewood. Although I had a few carved whale samples along, a different sea mammal took center stage on this day, as the boxes of carvings on board were mostly seals and sea lions.

On up the cliffs I went, to a promontory like no other that shrouded one of the world's largest sea caves. There, 300' above the roiling sea and the hollowed-out cave, perched a building. This was Sea Lion Caves, where I had a meeting scheduled to present my wares for their gift shop. To establish an account here would break me free to be an independent, full-time business: Pacific Carvings in Myrtlewood. The results of this meeting would dictate whether I could do it—or not.

The general manager, Steve Saubert, greeted me, sporting the hip afro trendy in the early 1980s. Steve appeared to be only slightly older than I, and we engaged easily in a discussion of my sea lion carvings as a potential addition to their shop. We hit it off well, perhaps due to an identity of shared values and styles, for I was sporting a full `fro as well.

At the end of the meeting, Steve encouraged me to visit the caves 300' below us to observe the sea lions close up. I relished this offer since it would help me with carving the details of the sea lions, and I thanked him for his generosity. While taking the swift elevator down to the cave floor, I recalled some long-ago images from my memory bank.

When my years could be counted on one hand, my father, "Dad Roy," had held that hand and guided me down a winding staircase that resembled the inside of a lighthouse. A scaffolding-like structure enclosing the staircase had been built on the side of the cliffs, for many years providing the only access down to view the sea lions inside their cave. Around and around, down, down we went in those fleeting images that I could remember, but I could never recall the climb back up. I am sure it was mostly on the shoulders of my father.

This immense cave hosted dozens upon dozens of stellar sea lions crowded together, with an opening to the sea that fully illuminated the unfolding scene. Most noticeably, an added pungency mixed into the salt spray air that only scores of animals weighing up to 1000 pounds could engender.

In the center of the cave one large pinnacle rock jutted up as the ocean waves swirled around it. Sea lions frolicked about on this mini island and jockeyed for positions as others slipped back into the churning waters. All the while, with lots of pushing and shoving, there was a constant struggle for dominance at the top of the promontory.

More sea lions crowded up against the rocky, steeply sloped back wall of the grotto. A safe distance away, an upper ledge served as a viewing platform for the human visitors encountering this wild and raucous melee in a natural marine environment.

With the ammo of a sea lion rendition I called "Sea Lion on the Rock" (and a matching afro), I had managed to seal the deal with the Sea Lion Caves manager, who belonged to the family that held ownership of the caves. Orders for my carvings followed.

Shortly before my meeting with Steve at the Caves, I had returned from a Rotary Club business exchange to Central Mexico, where I gave talks and presentations on the unique myrtlewood businesses of Southern Oregon, and showed samples of the carvings that made me a part of it. My slideshow also featured Bayview Manufacturing and much of its operations, since I still had one foot in that door. As the business exchange began winding down, I and the five other entrepreneurs in the program found ourselves in a place called Puerto Vallarta.

By this time, the agenda read something like "footloose and fancy free," which could have some questionable consequences in a seaside resort like Puerto Vallarta. At any rate, upon awakening late one morning, I glanced in the bathroom mirror and sighed, "Oh, I have an afro." It was the first and last time that I ever sat for a hair dresser and ordered up a perm. Could it have been the afro, however, that helped me turn the corner and nail down the account with Steve and the Sea Lion Caves? I'll never know, but I did know when it was time to let that `fro go.

Visiting the Mexican coast invited many opportunities to observe and sketch sea life. A session with the indigenous Seri peoples carving their stylized sea life in ironwood set a new tone for me. Watching sea lions on the rocks of the shorelines and the ironwood session gave me an infusion of inspiration, which resulted in the "Sea Lion on the Rock" carving back at my home studio.

This carving was in the mix of styles that I'd presented to Manager Steve at my Caves sales appointment, and stood out as a favorite. After this tenuous first step, the actual follow-ups and turnover of future sales would prove my true staying power with Sea Lion Caves.

Every summer on the Oregon Coast, tourism surges like a tidal wave through all the small towns, filling old town and dockside restaurants and bars to capacity. Galleries, gift shops, and other amusements abound, and, close at hand, recreation of all kinds are available for the choosing. Deep sea fishing, near shore crabbing, whale watching, beach combing, and mountain hiking all beckon coastal visitors. Everything pertaining to marine life and the oceanic atmosphere draws the attention of this wave of seaside enthusiasts.

This is the whole new world that opened up when I made my choice of relocating to the Oregon coast and working myrtlewood at Bayview. I explored the arts and crafts scene in local coastal hamlets and surveyed the possibilities of presenting my carvings. I scrutinized other artists' oceanic works and, early on, took particular notice of whale sketches on greeting cards by local artist Don McMichael. Seeing such work by others helped inspire my own artistic pursuits.

With my backyard shop and numerous sea animal and bird patterns of my own invention, I couldn't wait to grab the world by the tail and hang on for the ride. I jumped into this mainstream of commerce with my myrtlewood renditions of wildlife, carving a variety of subjects, but in this environment, sea life ruled supreme.

With an aggressive attempt to circulate my work to every myrtlewood shop north and south, and there were many, I became acquainted with all the shop proprietors and many myrtlewood workers and suppliers, and expanded my sales to other gift shops as well. Sea life carvings fit the coastal themes everywhere on the coast.

Once I produced an adequate supply of carved whales, seals, dolphins, pelicans, and other figures, I traveled Highway 101 to the many tourist locales to offer my wares wholesale to shop managers. Early on I relied on introductory cold calls, and by appointments once I'd established an account. Eventually most clients began to mail or phone in orders, which I shipped or hand delivered. The coast highway and its tourism paid off in sales.

While it's true that I had good luck with sales, as my work usually sold itself, it was not always the case. On one venture seeking outlets for my carvings, a fine furniture maker berated my carvings, criticizing the sanding of my works. "You don't even go down to a 400 grit sanding!" he high-handedly pointed out. He did not seem to understand that my 3-D figures of wildlife were all rounded and contoured, which takes a special sanding process to be effective. Also, many of my carvings were intentionally tool-marked to enhance details and for the special effect of texture.

Even though it was destined for fine furniture, this shop owner's pieces were flat work, boards if you will, that could benefit from flat sanding to the nth degree. I left his establishment disappointed with no sales, but still feeling comfortable with my level of standards that he hadn't fully appreciated.

Another bump in my early career road occurred when I supplied a coastal shop called the Myrtle Tree. While creating the gray whales, seals, and dolphins for their order, I used a generous amount of myrtle sapwood with its consistently solid gray tones. Because it matched the true gray colors of the sea animals so well, I readily produced the works and filled the order. However, in the wide range of myrtle colorations, gray is considered plain, and in the buying public's scrutinizing eye, the flashier grain patterns are more desirable.

After a disparaging letter of complaint and some personal jabs from the Myrtle Tree establishment, I made the commitment to always use the most colorful wood for orders, regardless of the true animal tones. However, I continued matching the color tones of wood to those of the animals when the animal and the wood were of a spectacular nature, such as tiger-stripe grain for tiger sharks.

What came about from my Sea Lion Caves venture was a long and fruitful business relationship, with years of orders that resulted in thousands of sea lions and seals carved from my hands and channeled out into the world as souvenirs of the caves. At Steve's request, I eventually designed a myrtlewood sea lion that replicated the logo of the caves. Dozens of these in various sizes were ordered as they became sought-after icons of the cliff top establishment. When the caves celebrated their 60th anniversary of the facility, marine artist Don McMichael and I were invited to exhibit our sea life art during the festivities.

In 1984, a new aquarium opened where you could watch sea otters bobbing in kelp beds from an observation deck or out the back windows of the building. Monterey Bay Aquarium in Monterey, California set a new precedent for cutting edge sea life experiences. Even before their announced opening, I made contact with the new facility. After making an appointment with their gift shop buyers and showing them my work, I received extended orders for my sea life carvings. I was especially flattered by receiving checks signed by Julie Packard, the daughter of a Hewlett Packard founding father and a major force behind the new marine facility.

My ability to expand Pacific Carvings continued to compound as I increased outlets for carvings and added new equipment. After I converted that old double-wide trailer house into an expansive workshop, my midlife career run hit full steam ahead. The Cadillac of my enterprise came in the form of a special order, eight-setting spindle carving machine. With this luxury tool I created a whole new line of North American animals. The course was set, and the results were moose, howling and pacing wolves, leaping deer, bull elk, bighorn ram on a precipice, and a bear with a salmon. I also expanded my sea life offerings with larger, more realistic seals and sea lions.

Using my individually carved originals for models, the hand-operated machine produced acceptable roughed out renditions in numbers. After the spindle carver roughouts came the complex re-carving over each piece with sanders and handheld burr grinders. In the final carving step, detailed work of the animal's features resulted in completed lifelike figurines.

Ramping up production meant circulating more carvings out into the world. I pursued outlets for my work throughout the western U.S. and across the nation. I sold moose in Alaska and sea life in Florida. North American wildlife carvings found their way to Crater Lake National Park and Multnomah Falls Recreation Area in Oregon. Sea World in Texas and Trees of Mystery in California carried my work; one-of-a-kind humpback whales and dolphins mounted on driftwood "waves" exhibited in galleries in Hawaii, Nantucket Island, Florida, and the coast of Oregon.

As part of a woodworkers co-op, I had the opportunity to participate in major gift shows in Seattle and Los Angeles, which generated dozens of orders and accounts, necessitating extra employees during busy summer months. I shipped my carvings to New York, New Jersey, Vermont,

Washington State islands, Jackson Hole in Wyoming, and other far-reaching locations.

Though I carried on working production carvings in large numbers, a desire to create a higher level of art pieces for galleries fomented in my being. This artwork came slowly, since little time could be reserved for this pursuit, and the blind blur of producing carvings was needed for raising my family. Determination paid off, however, when my art pieces created on the side found homes, first on the local coast scenes and then farther afield. My evolution as an artist had set its course, with the elevation of free-form wildlife and sea life sculptures to the level of fine art as my ultimate goal. Initially, the resources that I relied on for this realm of work came from pockets of driftwood scattered around the vast Coos Bay.

Watersheds are just that: torrents of seasonal accumulation that shed stumps, roots, and whole trees, and wash them all downstream until they are deposited into the bay. Driftwood piles up in pockets dictated by currents, resulting in a wood artist's gold mine of weathered wood in all shapes and forms. Although myrtle comprised a small percentage of the various species in the mix, I learned to identify it by sight and found much of it to be extraordinary material for artwork.

The turning point began one Thanksgiving weekend when river flood waters had receded from weeks of relentless rainfall. My corner of the bay, normally shallow mud flats, had become layered with new driftwood so thick you could walk 100' or more out during low tide. Pawing through the heaps of driftwood, I came away with potential swooping eagles, emerging salmon, and other figures of artistic flair from mountain sources conveniently deposited close to home. Using my carving tools to bring these envisioned figures to life in free-form art pieces meant years of satisfying work.

Late one Easter afternoon, after family festivities died down and our three children had cached their share of Easter eggs, I hit upon a new carving concept. Following the lines and forms of a driftwood hollow log segment, I first chalked in the features of swimming salmon to follow the curve of the rounded, hollow shape. Then, with a chainsaw, I cut away much of the log for the salmon and enhanced the rustic lower half to support the piece, leaving the parts joined on this natural driftwood base. When the shaping and detail work was finished, I had two fully curving salmon to show for my efforts.

Thus began my experimental work of life-sized, radically curving salmon cut from hollow logs from the forest. This process included sealing the end grain of the salmon slices and carefully air drying them for at least a year. Eventually, I worked up some salmon that were almost touching head-to-tail in a 360° circle.

Soon, I had fine-tuned my new line to include these single salmon swimming through rustic, all natural loops of darkened myrtle acquired from roots and stumps with their hollowed-out formations. The long-term demand for my new signature works was the ultimate payoff of an experiment gone right.

Extensive myrtle stands lined the riverside campground at Laverne Park on the North Fork Coquille River and were scattered throughout the park, including many gnarled giants with hollow trunks and others leaning with sagging branches. Within the not-so-distant past there had been a fatality in the campground when a large limb had fallen on some unlucky soul. "Fatality" is a crisp, clean word, impersonal at best, and in this case used to describe someone who'd been tragically squished by a tree.

Once the Bureau of Land Management wisely determined it would be best to avoid future liability on land they owned, a clean-up project to remove hazardous trees lurking about the park ensued. Tree experts deemed more than two dozen unruly trees as threats to this public playground and marked them to be purged. Almost all were myrtles dotted around the camp sites, with some Doug fir giants in the mix to help pay the bills. In the dead of winter, timber fallers and a local, modest-sized cutting mill were contracted for this major off-season overhaul of the park.

The melee that followed was like pirates unloading on a virgin island, with chainsaws (including mine) replacing cutlasses, and front-end loaders bearing away the wealth of wood. A giant monarch of Doug fir in the very center of the park was also marked for felling, even though the stump, measuring 9' across, looked as sound as the day it was born, which happened to be over 300 years ago. I personally measured the tree and counted the annual rings, and discovered no apparent decay.

I arrived on the scene after most of the trees had been fallen. Firewood haulers had trailers stacked to the hilt, premium fir logs were being hauled to the small local mill, and front-end loaders were shoving and piling logs about. Since many of the hazard trees were hollow myrtles, it translated into gravy time for me, because nobody wanted to deal with the hollow trunks and hollow burl mounds—not even the firewood cutters. BLM simply wanted it cleared, and I found myself with free reign to salvage as much as I could haul away.

My old Weyerhaeuser faller's saw with a 42" bar was my weapon of choice, and I worked it for three days of selective cutting. The rewards were a generous supply of curved salmon, rustic hollows, burl formations, and the future satisfaction of giving new life to a wondrous material that would otherwise be laid waste. Within the next handful of years, I had circulated dozens of major art works from this source throughout America's Pacific Coast, from Southern California to Alaska.

With due respect to the Coos County Parks department that manages the campground and the BLM that owns the land, time has ensured recovery from the aggressive tree removal impact, and the average camper today would not recognize the loss of any monolithic myrtles. The river and its campsites remain lined with their share of sheltering, hobbit-flavored shade trees.

Myrtlewood Wildlife Art,
The Process, by Terry J. Woodall

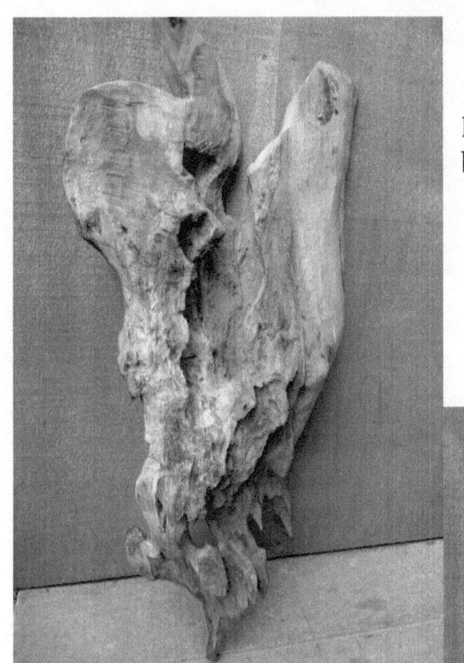

Myrtlewood stump-root section before carving work begins.

Carving completed on one heron.

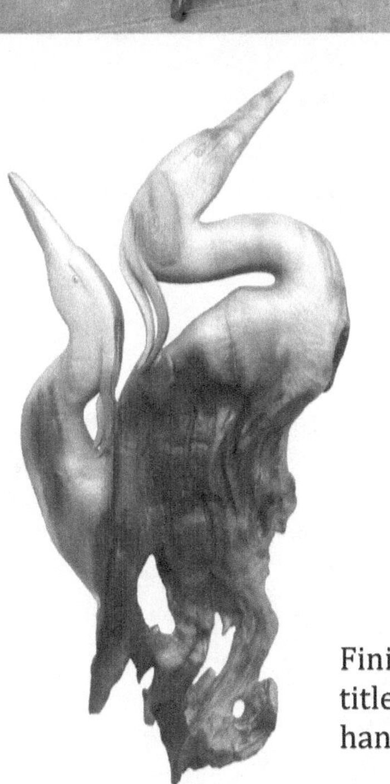

Finished free-form wall piece titled "Entwined" ready for hanging. H38" x W24"

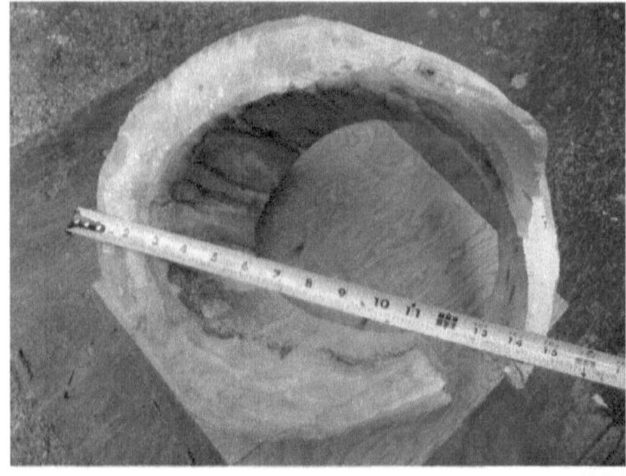

Chainsaw-cut round from hollow myrtlewood log. After 2 years of controlled air drying, rough-out begins.

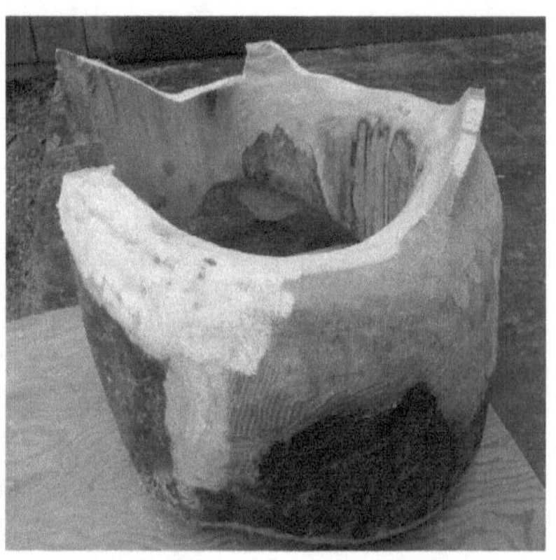

Carving out the salmon, shaping of fins and tail.

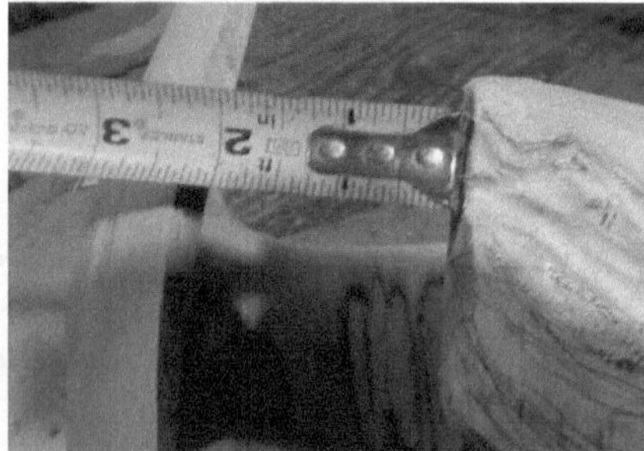

Face-mouth outlined, distance between head and tail noted. Salmon hollow is almost a full circle.

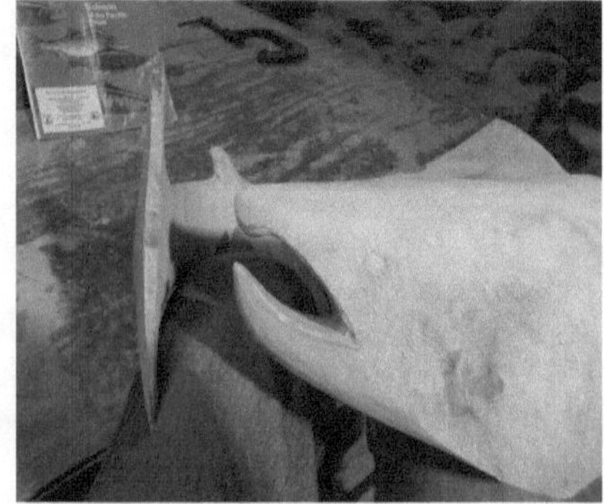

Mouth carved out, tail thinned.

Finished salmon sculpture mounted around rustic base, also of myrtlewood. Circular length of fish, 39."

"Head to Tail," H33" x W16"
Photos of finished piece by Memo Jasso

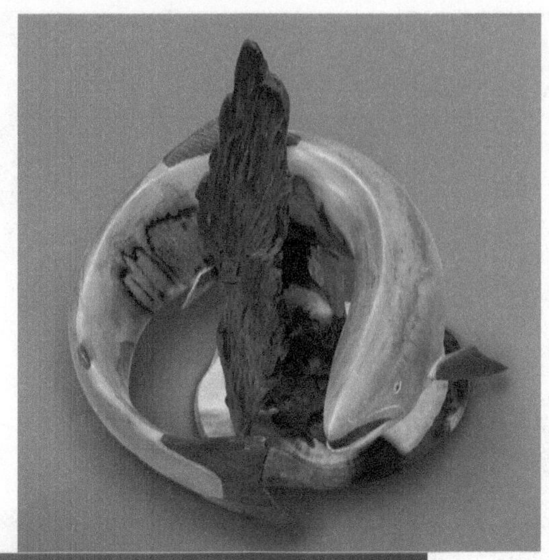

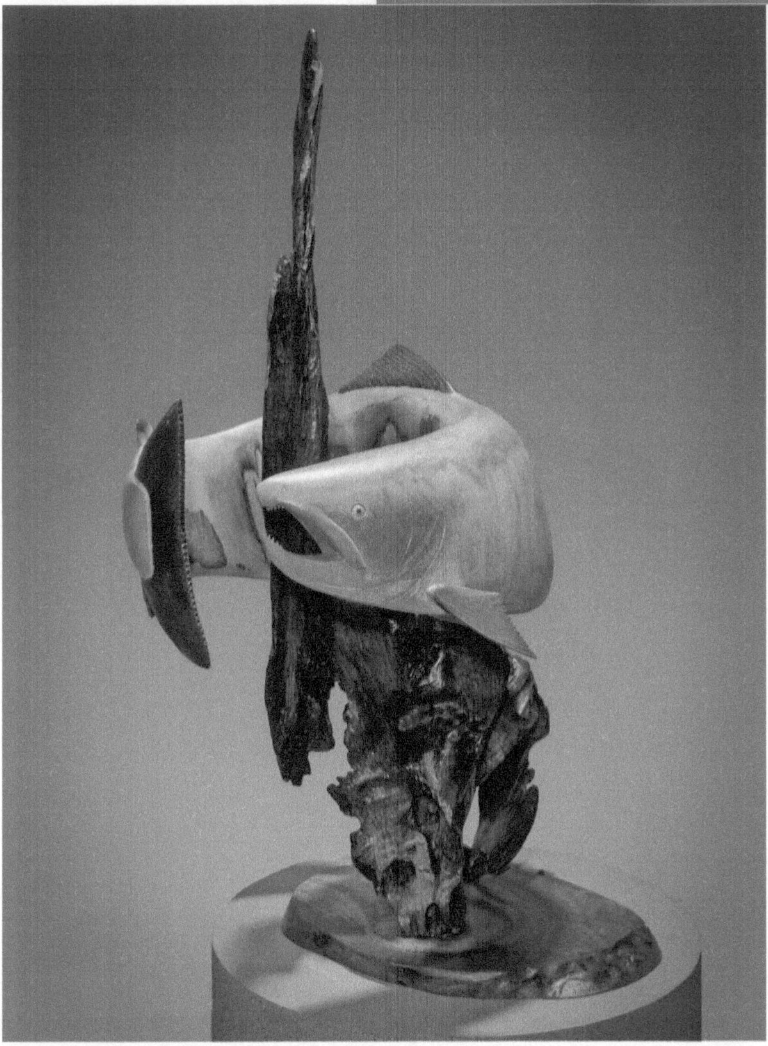

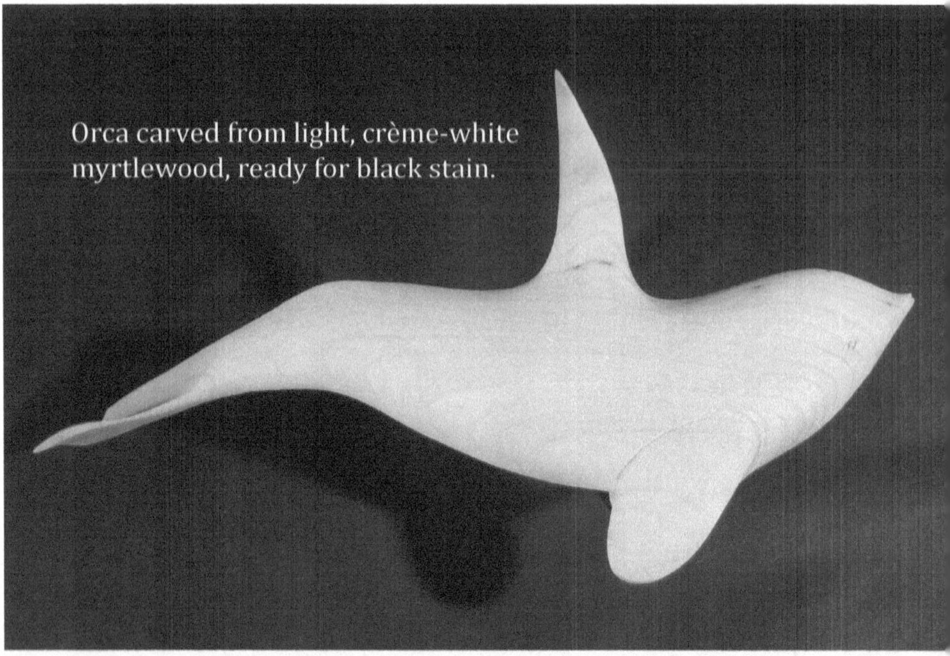

Orca carved from light, crème-white myrtlewood, ready for black stain.

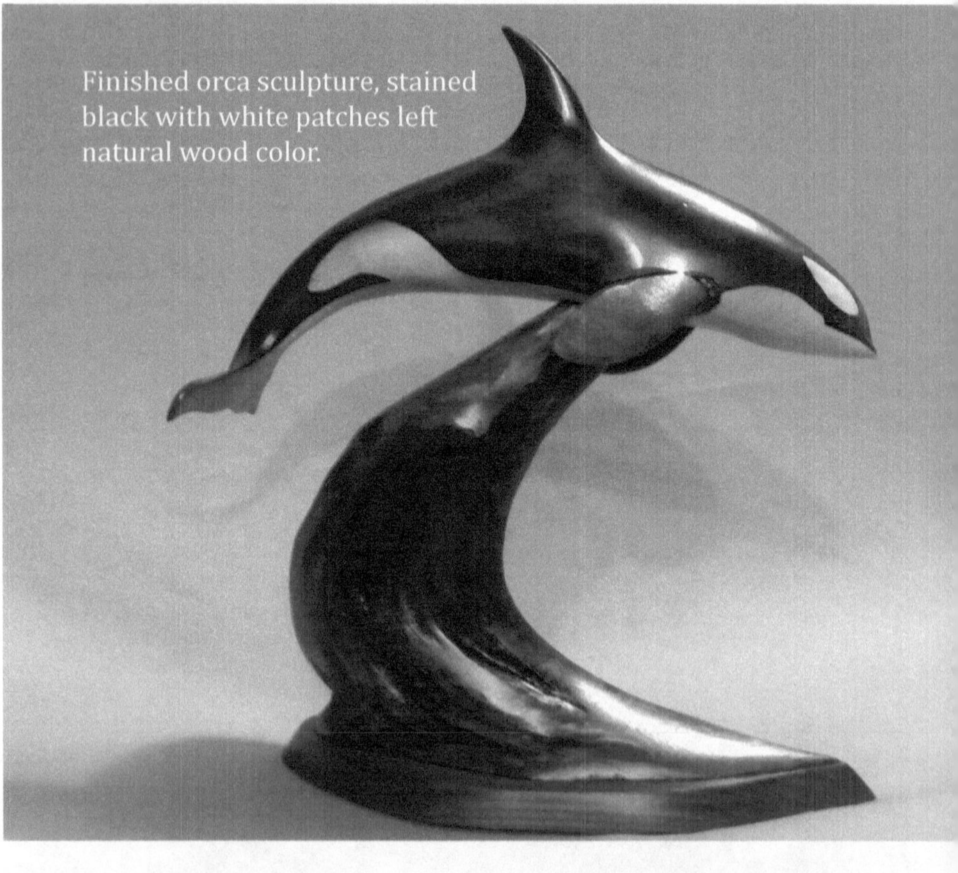

Finished orca sculpture, stained black with white patches left natural wood color.

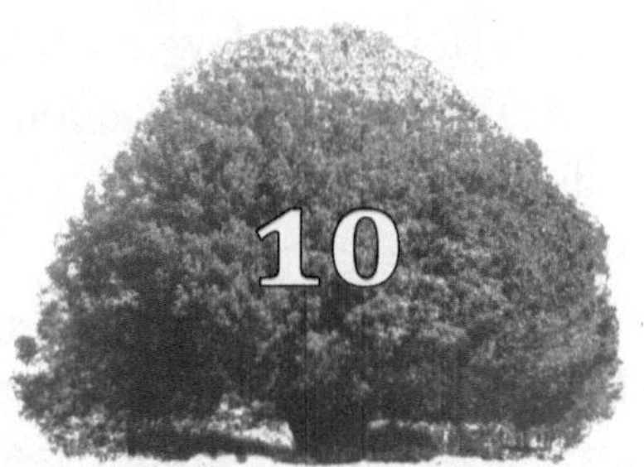

10

Celebrating the Green & Blue

In a burst of enthusiasm, the affable woman shook the sprig of green towards her rapt listeners as if it were something marvelous. She then proclaimed the myrtle leaves to be a "bit o' the green" to represent the first Coos Bay Area myrtle festival that would coincide with St. Patrick's Day, which happened to land on a weekend in March of 1985.

This dark-haired, high-octane gal was named Carol Berg, and Carol stayed firmly at the helm as the festival plans unfolded. The planning meeting that she addressed drew an audience of local myrtlewood workers and shop owners eager to be on board with the brainstorming of festival possibilities. What a great shot in the arm this would be for local myrtlewood crofters, setting myrtlewood and their products front row and center.

B. Roger Clark looked dapper in his blue suit jacket as he always did on important business occasions, and assumed a seat of honor befitting his myrtlewood empire. Dan and Carol Scoville were hands-on representing Barber Baskets, and Scott West stood in for the stoic House of Myrtlewood. The businesses of Heritage Myrtlewood, G & B Myrtlewood, and Bill Leslie with his Nature's Wooden Image store in Pony Village Mall were all part of the program, along with my Pacific Carvings.

Under the umbrella of the Greater Bay Area Tourism Council, Carol Berg & Co. was assigned to reel in a fishing net full of coastal town jewels and promote them with festivals. Music makers, whale migrations, myrtle trees...all reflected the string of municipalities surrounding Coos Bay that were ready to sing their merits. Hence the festival's official title: Bay Area Festival of the Myrtle Tree.

Carol Berg already had ads in the works promising free keepsakes for all festival goers, a "Wearin' o' the Green" commemorative green ribbon combined with myrtle leaf clusters. "Combining the festival with St. Paddy's Day struck me as a great time to celebrate a little greenery," she said with a wink, "with a free keepsake to ward off St. Paddy's Day pinches!"

Suggestions from the group for the keepsakes' wording included lines like "Begorrah! I was at the Myrtle Fest!" Our newly formed festival committee focused on a two-pronged exhibit for the ambitious weekend festival with craft booths planned for display in the Pony Village Mall and more elaborate artworks to be viewed in the Coos Art Museum. All of us stepped in, taking on as much as we could handle to make this the best festival ever.

You might remember the days when shopping malls swarmed with people all day, every day, and served as indisputable community centers. Hence, it made sense that the main hub of festival activities would be centered there.

To ensure easy access, the event committee scheduled a shuttle van service from the mall to the local myrtlewood factories for facility tours and to the Coos Art Museum for its exhibits.

The luck of the Irish rubbed off on the festival everywhere, as Ms. Berg was a zealous organizer, planning live music and dancing, refreshments, and a wealth of advertising. Since myrtle's edibility was well known both for the fruit of its nuts and its pungent leaves that can be used in herbal teas, planned refreshments included dried and ground leaves made into popcorn seasoning, tea, and baked into cookies.

When the time came for Carol to assign a volunteer to plug the festival on a local "People Show," I found she was looking directly at me. "Terry!"

"Why's everybody looking at me?" I protested. Everyone laughed. "Of course I'll do it," I said, knowing that I was infamous for my insuppressible enthusiasm for all things myrtlewood.

Finally, with the exhibition venues and factory tours confirmed, I still felt that something was missing. Why couldn't there be an informative presentation that covered all things myrtlewood? I hit upon "A Stroll Down Myrtlewood Lane," a walkway that would wind through exhibits in a large meeting hall and open up to the main aisle of the mall, where booths for shops and producers were planned. In a later meeting, I was applauded for my idea and given a free hand to make it happen.

The first stop on our whimsical myrtle lane stroll displayed 50 million-year-old myrtle leaf fossils, petrified myrtlewood, and tree ring cross sections from ancient trees with their ages noted. The first explanatory sign read

"Myrtle's been around for a long, long time." To each side of the pathway, boughs of fresh green myrtle were woven around display edges, winding up structural posts of the mall, and leading on down the "lane."

The next stop highlighted "Myrtle in Nature," featuring actual wood samples illustrating the tree's many unusual forms of growth. This included cross sections of the tree's reaction to wood pecker strikes and wood rat gnawings, samples of burl formations and complete circles created from natural grafts, and clusters of "grape" burls and other unique tree wood pieces. Large photos of the tree and its groves brought the outdoors inside for a sense of realism.

"In Our History" consisted of photos depicting activities in working myrtlewood over the years, with displays of antiques, and photos and texts highlighting early shops and their founding fathers. This stop naturally continued into "In the Community" and "In the Home," which included everything from ship wheels and church crosses to spinning wheels and furniture. Since the majority of myrtlewood products tend to be turned bowls and similar implements, "In the Kitchen" stood out as a prominent feature.

"In the Factory" relied on a slide show projected on a wall screen to unveil the inner workings of a myrtlewood factory. To prepare for my earlier Rotary Club business exchange to Mexico, I had taken a photographer on a tour of Bayview Manufacturing to compile a behind-the-scenes overview of myrtlewood in production. The same slide show fit nicely into the myrtle lane stroll.

"In Our Imaginations" rounded out our stroll with a wealth of carvings and other imaginative renderings in myrtlewood on display. Needless to say, I loaded up this exhibit with art from the Pacific Carvings workshop. There were also many imaginative and decorative touches added to the layout of the entire stroll.

To my amazement, Roger Clark brought in a special portable cabinet with a complete set of carved animal miniatures, myrtlewood figurines that measured 1-2" in different dimensions. At least three dozen realistic wildlife renditions peeked out from the cabinet, which opened up into its own display case. This was a monumental addition to the "Imagination" display, most notably because it was created by one of the best master carvers in myrtlewood history, and a true pioneer of the art form, Bob Harbison.

According to an early 1970's *Oregonian* newspaper article, at 68 years old, Bob Harbison laid claim to having designed and produced more than 100,000 carvings of various myrtlewood animals, fish, and birds. Most of his realistic carvings were substantial desktop-sized figures, not miniatures like those in Roger's display case. Many of the animals produced at Bayview that I had learned to carve were his prototypes, indicating that Roger had singular access to Harbison's works near the end of his days.

This master carver's original kingly elephants graced the desks of both President Richard Nixon and President Ronald Reagan, who were, of course, both Republican elephant fans. More than 50 of Harbison's carved elephants were sent to Washington, D.C. by representatives of the Oregon Republican Party.

Though I never met the man, Harbison was my main mentor and his works my first inspirations for carving wildlife in myrtlewood. Harbison passed away from cancer about the same time that I first laid eyes on those carved elephants at Bayview's original shop, prototypes of the presidential elephants (carved by Roger's employees using Harbison's models, not by Harbison himself). I have continued to carve various renditions based on those same elephant carvings I had once produced at Bayview.

There are many ways to make a basket, but if you were a wooden boat builder for most of your life and decided to make a basket from myrtlewood, odds are good that this basket would be sturdy and impervious to the erosion of time. Another attention-getter of the festival emerged from displays of these old-fashioned-style "Barber Baskets."

This builder of boats named Don Barber came from the seafaring village of Charleston, and had turned his baskets into a family enterprise in 1979. His daughter Carol and son-in-law Dan Scoville eventually expanded the business into nationwide sales, offering about eight selections of various sizes and styles assembled by hand from 2"-wide thin strips of multi-colored myrtlewood and copper tacks. There is even a dory-shaped basket, hearkening back to the enterprise's seafaring roots.

At one point, even Martha Stewart got in on the act with an executive gift basket line for Ralph Lauren using Barber picnic baskets that were featured in many home decor magazines. As of 2022, these desirable creations are still being produced in Charleston by Don Barber's son Greg.

Our Myrtlewood Festival revived an interest in holding meetings for all comers involved in the industry. The annual weekend festival entertained the public and broadcast the virtues of our homegrown tree on a four-year run. When it phased out, the vacuum left by the festival was destined to be filled with a new focus; myrtle groves in parks.

Curiously, a former and more formal Association had staged a mini-mart in Pony Village on the same weekend in March, only nine years earlier. The 1976 event was billed as a bicentennial celebration effort, with myrtlewood items for sale and collections on display.

This official Myrtlewood Association was established in January, 1967 and included elected officers, dues, and scheduled meetings. This organization lasted well into the late `70s, and after it disbanded a loosely formed version of the association continued to meet whenever a project of mutual interest arose, such as the Myrtlewood Festival. This informal group included owners of myrtlewood establishments, both shops and producers, who kept the spirit and identity alive, but dropped regular meetings. A scattering of shops throughout the state not located in the myrtle rich commerce of the Southern Oregon Coast also participated in myrtlewood-related activities.

Although a motivating Carol Berg propelled the Myrtlewood Festival along for a number of years, that wasn't the only festival in her repertoire. A few years after the first celebration of the myrtle "green" came the whale "blue," a March spin-off into a new Whale Festival. *The whales are migrating! Come see the whales! Celebrate the whales! Save the whales!*

Save the Whales, one of the earliest environmental slogans used in the push for wildlife conservation, resonated in the early `60s and on. With this same enthusiasm, Coos Bay's pacific locality introduced the Whale Festival to coincide with the annual spring migration of gray whales. Locally, optimum viewing opportunities abounded for this species that had been successfully protected and was enjoying rebounding numbers.

Carol brought the festival to the whales, presenting a whale-themed art show strategically located close to the whale watching shoreline, where I was invited to show my myrtlewood sea life. The excitement was infectious; no one was immune. "Where's the whale art show? Are we at the right place?" one young couple, beaming in the late morning sunshine, asked me as I came and went from the venue. "We just flew in from Hawaii. We came to see Don's latest work."

"You're at the right place," I assured them, nodding towards the old coastguard boathouse. I thought about Don McMichael's whale paintings in Hawaii galleries and what an impact the paintings must have, to generate such a following that people were willing to fly six hours across an ocean to see his new work!

An unlikely spot for the location of an art show, the old coastguard boathouse was tucked away at the end of the sand, cobbled to the rock ledges and giant boulders that jutted into the bay. For several decades it had served as a launching pad to rescue mariners in distress, with its easy visual of the jetties guarding the opening into the vast ocean. A half mile across the water from the strategically placed building stretched a sand spit many miles long that abruptly ended where the bay finally surged into the Pacific.

Once you found yourself there, it was easy to see how the pristine venue was perfect for a display of marine art. Polished wood floors and walls of windows merged the spacious main hall with the restless bay and its barrage of sea birds, and whale bones greeted visitors in the lobby. Though the building had been remodeled into a lecture hall, adjoining a marine biology campus, the lifeboat launching skids still receded into the water.

Bright and early, I was bringing my carved myrtlewood sea life into the exhibit hall when a fellow pulled up in a pickup with Colorado plates, jumped out, and began a frantic conversation. "Where are the whales," he asked excitedly, "how can I see them? Where is the whale art?" Again, I directed the visitor to the boathouse, but he suddenly seemed more interested in the orca whales I was carrying in my arms. "I don't think I have time to see the whales," he went on as he glanced at his watch, and then eyeing the carved orcas, "and I really can't wait for the show to open, but I would sure like to take one of those home with me."

The orca collection was one of my early experiments with black staining on plain white myrtlewood to highlight the markings of the striking animals, a technique that eventually evolved into renditions that became widely popular. I'd also sought out natural driftwood forms that resembled waves, cleaned them up, and added gray stain where needed. These driftwood waves made perfect oceanic bases for displaying the orcas and other sea life, and were making their debut here along with the new orca staining techniques.

Although outside "parking lot" sales at art events are questionable, I made sure the festival was commissioned for my early morning sale. I knew I'd made the right decision when I saw the delighted expression on the Coloradan's face once he knew the whale replica from this edge of the world was leaving with him for the mountain state. Without visiting the festival art show, he turned around his pickup and left with his newly found prize.

Once again I was reminded of the impact our omnipresent yet elusive ocean dwellers have on humans. Part of the mystical power of the sea is that we know busy cities of life flourish just below this sheet of blue-gray nothingness. It is the majestic whale that surfaces to remind us of those cities.

Only three artists were selected for the art show segment of the Whale Festival: Don McMichael, whale painter, Jo Barton, artist of local shoreline landscapes, and myself, carver of myrtlewood whales, dolphins, and seals. I announced myself as the "new kid on the block" as I set up with these seasoned and much proclaimed artists, although mine was a much different block since they painted and I worked wood in the round. Thrilled to be exhibiting in this marine environment, I set up displays of my sea life renditions, many of which were mounted on driftwood waves, and greeted the opening with optimism after my parking lot sale.

Don paints whales, whales of all species: breaching whales, whales under the sea, whales with dolphins, whales with sailing ships, arctic whales in ice floes, tropical whales with palms, whales with sea lions and sea birds. Underwater perspectives combined with above water views fill most of his canvases, with translucent blues and greens surrounding the sea mammal subjects.

An ex-Coast Guard officer, Don's studio is an endless delight of sea faring memorabilia, from narwhal tusks to ship wheels and lanterns, to an extensive collection of glass floats of all sizes, most originating from his own forays on local beaches. My own career has benefited greatly by my inspirational visits and discussions with this marine artist at his studio.

In contrast to the undersea world of whales, Jo Barton focused on the shorelines, scenes of sand and water. I first knew Jo Barton as quiet and unassuming in the local mall shows, content to put her work out there and eager to share it with all comers. I was immediately enthralled by her images, and unabashedly favored her work for the simple reason that she painted and captured the mood of my favorite local surroundings: rugged cliffs holding back the turbulent ocean, soft waves meeting driftwood logs, and the sprinkle of wildflowers over brushy shorelines.

Driven by her passion for the environment's natural beauty, Jo's formula was simple: to recreate local nature scenes with soft pastels. Her paintings encompassed a quiet realism, such that one could almost hear and feel the rise and fall of the gentle surf washing over the wrinkled sand. From a quote in her own bio, Jo enthused, "I hope to someday soon live in a small motor home that's all windows. No housework or gardening, just painting and living—what a way to go!"

Jo Barton's work was eminently recognizable. On a fishing trip in Alaska, for example, my son Josh and I were thrown in with a guide of Asian descent and a seafood connoisseur from Kentucky. The Kentuckian took home a 150-pound halibut for his landlubber's sea food club, while Josh and I settled for a few nice salmon and the excitement of humpback whales cruising the channels we navigated. Naturally, whale sightings and observations are important technical and inspirational tools for my artistic endeavors, and always a thrill.

Wet and tired from the long day on the sea, the kindly expert guide invited us to recoup at his home a short distance off dockside. As his equally hospitable wife served up hot coffee and snacks, I noticed a familiar-looking painting hanging from their wall. "That looks just like a scene from our area, and could even be by an artist I know."

"That's because it is," the guide's wife beamed back at me, knowing we were from Coos Bay. "It's by my aunt, Jo Barton, who's from your home town." So began an enthusiastic conversation with a "small world" flair, extolling Jo's talent to capture the look and feel of the misty northwest coast that were equally fitting for Alaska.

Some years later, after the fervor of the Whale Festival, and after many more carved myrtlewood whales had left my hands, a news listing of a Jo Barton retrospective at a local gallery caught my attention. I eagerly sought out her exhibit, and immersed myself in her pastel renditions of familiar nature scenes and backwater haunts. From room to room I wandered, until I reached the last small alcove harboring her last lonely painting. A thunderbolt shook me as the painting leaped out until it seemed to fill the entire wall. There were no calm beaches with lapping waves, no light and whimsical flowers. All tranquility had been stripped away.

The mental rays of sunshine that brightened most of her paintings had been supplanted by a terrifying tempest that challenged the last stand of a solitary black rock rising out of the abyss. Equally dark, unforgiving seas raged and tore at the lonely sea stack, a symbolic outpost attempting to withstand the storm venting from the night sky.

This was Jo Barton's final painting, the first and last dark cloud coming from the brush of this serene lady, painted as she wrestled with the unyielding grips of an illness that prematurely took away her life of pastel colors.

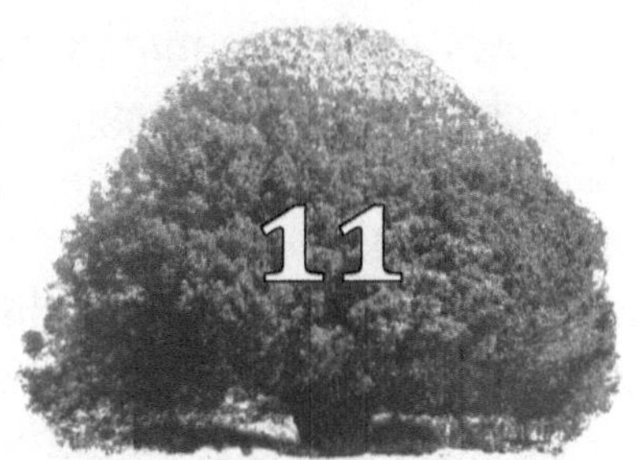

11

Owls & Japan

After I'd been absent from Bayview Manufacturing for a handful of years, a sales opportunity opened up when Bayview needed carved owls to supply a lucrative outlet in Japan. The lure of Oregon's myrtlewood had infatuated an entrepreneur from that Asian country who'd opened his own shop to sell myrtlewood. Bayview was his main supplier.

B. Roger Clark supplied me with the specs for the rounded owl head statuettes, and we agreed on a dozen different sizes of an identical model and negotiated prices. Working with Roger as an independent supplier after four years of being a hired hand was gratifying indeed.

When all lined up in a row, the owls made an impressive stair step from the very smallest height (1-1/2") to the largest (16"). I created hundreds of them to fill steady orders at a good profit. We rode this wave of success for many months until the orders stalled due to circumstances beyond my control.

I approached Roger's office one morning to contest some overdue payments on a batch of owls. As I waited… and waited…I realized this was likely one of those times when a major player wants to intimidate a rival across the desk to gain a psychological advantage, and this was the first predictable step: the waiting game, one of the well-used tricks in the playbook.

The receptionist finally opened the door into Roger's office, and I sat down across from his desk where I became the recipient of the next move. I waited longer as Roger shuffled a bunch of papers and avoided eye contact. Finally, he looked up to greet me with a drawn out, "Mr. Ooou-dall," in the tone of someone who had just stepped in a dog pile. This was a man who knew my name and its pronunciation perfectly well. After all, I'd known him for years. I said nothing. Humiliation tactics would not deter me from my objective.

When it comes to matters of money, particularly money owed, combat readiness and a stiffened spine usually develops in short order. After a bit of routine jousting, however, I left dissatisfied. The owl orders dried up, and, though I was eventually paid for my work, my connection to Japan had dissolved.

It was quite some time before I saw Roger again, and when I did he had sold the company and begun coasting into retirement. Bayview Manufacturing became simply the Myrtlewood Factory. After assisting in the transition to the new ownership, Roger arranged for unlimited use of the shop floor for his own projects. Beautifully crafted blanket chests were his focus, and it was easy to see that he was enjoying the woodworking without the stress of ownership and bottom lines.

Years earlier, Roger's gift shop segment of the factory had been changed from the long standing Myrtlewood Chalet to an emphatic Real Oregon Gift title with the slogan "Nature's Gift to Oregon, Oregon's Gift to You." This pointed in the right direction, for many myrtlewood products region-wide were purchased in the spirit of gift giving. The new owners wisely retained The Real Oregon Gift banner for their gift shop.

The gift shop had also been integrated into a corner of the spacious factory building from the earlier log cabin shop nearby. One afternoon I was lining up my carved seals and whales on the gift shop counter for a sales review when Roger came in from the factory with a freshly minted blanket chest. Just as the owner and I were negotiating prices for my carvings, from across the room Roger looked us over, glanced at my carvings on the counter, and proudly exclaimed, "I taught him everything he knows!"

It was then that I knew Roger still felt invested in my progression as a myrtlewood artist. He did not own an overly expressive personality, and was someone who kept his poker hand close to his chest, so this expression of pride was rare. Yes, you may have taught me many tools of the trade and the guiding principles of working myrtlewood, I thought, but not quite everything!...and I returned to sales of my carvings.

In a certain Native American tongue, *Hoquiam* translates to "wood-hungry people," and it is also the name of a coastal town in neighboring Washington State. Although this name originated well outside myrtlewood territory, it still resonates with all forested Pacific slopes and its wood-dependent communities. The port of Coos Bay is no different, with its share of wood-hungry people that justified its existence, including those that shined a light on myrtlewood.

If wood-hungry people inhabit the Pacific Northwest of America, wood-reverent people inhabit the country of Japan, which I discovered first hand. I had just learned that the door to my relationship with Japan had not fully closed, as I had previously believed, when I found myself on a sister city business exchange between Coos Bay, Oregon and Choshi, Japan.

After flying past Mount Fujiyama and dropping into the country with our local representatives, I strolled neighborhoods on quiet back streets, noting the Japanese reverence for wood apparent in the centuries-old wooden shrines and small temples interspersed among cedar homes. An aura of devoted craftsmanship hung over the heavy, hand-hewn timbers with their intricate joints, along with carved dragons and other caricatures that peered from the sweeps of the eaves.

At Choshi's main event, I had the role of the exhibiting artist representing the Coos Bay area and its myrtlewood. In the large exhibit hall, Oregon products lined the shelves and tables at booths for our host's business/cultural exchange presentations. My very good friend and expert winemaker, Phil Gale, manned a nearby booth showcasing Southern Oregon wines. We were the foreigners, along with the rest of our entourage, and all the locals in attendance seemed pleased with our offerings.

My myrtlewood sculptures of elk and whales, dolphins and sea birds, seals and sea lions, were all exhibited at this evening highlight of the week-long program, but carvings from the black myrtlewood sawn by Lloyd Bechtel drew the most attention from the crowd. Reverence for wood began to shine even brighter.

"Mastah piece, your mastah piece!" came one emphatic request from a modest and solitary presence that appeared at my exhibit. It took a few moments before I understood why this man, standing in the midst of a virtual myrtlewood forest of creations, was not looking at any of them. He wanted my "masterpiece."

I quickly appraised the situation. I had no one piece designated as a "masterpiece," but would do my best to offer this customer a piece of great stature aligned with quality workmanship and the accompanying price tag indicating its value. In the blink of an eye, I directed him to a magnificent whale mounted on my signature wave action driftwood. The large 30" whale was fully carved in black myrtlewood, the rarest form of a rare wood, and I assumed the man, obviously an aficionado of fine woods, would be pleased.

I was therefore surprised and taken aback when he balked at my offering and stepped away. "I will relay this news to my associate," he said soberly, and then exited into a hall through a nearby side door. I wondered if I'd ever see him again.

People aren't always that predictable, however, and before long the man was back, sidling over to me as though we were about to exchange state secrets and urging me into a corner of my art display area. Looking around to make sure our backs faced the busy traffic of the exhibit hall, he produced a roll of Japanese yen, and with a maximum amount of concealment, quickly peeled off bills until he had paid me in full for the whale sculpture. It seemed, after conferring with the buyer in the hall, whom I never met, that the only requirement of his sight-unseen purchase was that it be my "masterpiece." Without a doubt, this transaction still stands out as the most unusual sale of my entire career.

When the exhibit drew to a close, I retired to my host family's home giddy from the unpredictable evening. Entering the cozy sitting room, I found the grandmother of the house sitting on pillows and busily slurping from a soup bowl (slurping was good manners in this part of the world). With her feet dangling into the customary fire pit in the floor beneath the large, low-lying table, this esteemed elder of the Sakurai family appeared to be in total comfort.

My curiosity was drawn to a glint of gold from a large opening into the adjoining room, and she nodded a welcome to explore the room. As I marveled at the extravagant gilded altar and ancient cabinetry in the center of this room, the college-age daughter with a wedding on the horizon appeared and shared an account of this Buddhist shrine, the soul of their home. This house had been recently built after the razing of the 500-year-old former structure that had housed the family for many generations. The sanctuary room, which contained fixtures preserved from the old house, and from the one before that, had remained intact. In keeping with their traditions, the new house had been built around it.

This is where the family paid homage to its ancestors with a high shelf that ran continuously around the room, holding the urns of their deceased, together with a painted portrait or photograph, depending on the era of their passing. This spiritually interconnected circle of ancestors, with the living family represented by the shrine in the center, would connect to future generations as well.

As my gaze swept around and around the room, taking in one urn after another, and the empty spaces for future use, the daughter's willing narrative helped me grasp the concept of this culture's life-overlapping-death philosophy. The Zen conscience is like holding hands through the ages, each generation gaining comfort that they, too, will be upheld by the succeeding family lineage. The perception prevailed that those who passed on stayed an integral part of the living family, and were really not gone at all.

In preparation for this sister city exchange to Japan, I had received a request from its Coos Bay coordinator to create a myrtlewood art piece representing our state and region for the mayor of Choshi. "Something significant to hang in his office," the coordinator said, "to present as a gift from our community." I'd jumped at the opportunity, immediately envisioning the exact piece for the occasion: the iconic official state animal embellishing our state flag, the beaver.

All woodcarvers know that throwing away "scraps" of wood is not always a good idea. When sawing logs and stumps I set aside unusual slices of exterior tree wood formations that would otherwise be waste. When trees build up layers of scar tissue over old wounds and hollows, the result of such "aberrant" growth can be compelling. All it takes is being in tune with the natural expressions by carefully peeling the bark away from these exterior forms to reveal an array of textures and shapes.

Triggered by the characteristics of these concave and convex flowing, natural surfaces, I often utilized them to match the anatomy of animals, producing lifelike and highly unique free-form figures for my repertoire of art pieces. When these pieces dry and age, they can turn very dark, almost black, and polish into an eye-catching finish.

It was while I was pondering over one of these remnants that I envisioned its potential for a carved beaver, particularly noting the striking, unusual zigzag of ridges that perfectly matched the texture of the animal's tail. The head shape, complete with a laid-back ear, and the body shape, all jumped out at me. With some careful carving of legs, forelegs, and paws, the figure took shape. An expressive face carved with the beaver's signature gnawing teeth rounded out this interpretation of natural tree wood.

The idea for framing this naturalistic image came just as easily. After cutting out an exact outline of our Oregon map from a flat, 14" x 14" myrtlewood panel, I sanded it smooth and attached the flat-backed beaver in the center. The wall art was ready for hanging! How could I not be excited at the prospect of presenting such a gift to the mayor of Chosi, Japan?

At the ceremony of good will, I joined our group's leaders and a scattering of participants as we crowded into the mayor's office. The mayor's face lit up when the carving was unveiled and he quizzically noted the carved beaver at its center. I was not sure he'd ever seen a beaver before, but the many "*hais*" and bows let us know that the gift had been well received. After the ceremony, the beaver state map in myrtlewood was shared with the public in a glass display case in the lobby before it found its final place hanging in the mayor's office.

Phil Clausen's old general store-turned-studio was flanked by a spreading, open bottomland that bustled with activity on a mild spring day. The fresh, aromatic green of this grassy field gently sloped to the nearby banks of the Coquille River, which had widened out as it neared its meeting with the Pacific Ocean. Wood Meister Clausen was all set to host the visiting entourage from the city of Shobu, Japan, with tables showcasing a cross section of regional arts and products on display in the nearby field.

Another Phil, my friend and Wine Meister Phil Gale, who had also been part of the Choshi exchange, had organized this mini-fair to entertain the Asian visitors and their American hosts, all part of the Roseburg-Shobu sister city program. Phil knew Clausen's impressive wood sculpted furnishings were sure to be a hit with the visitors from across the Pacific Ocean, and had invited me to coordinate my myrtlewood wildlife sculptures into the program. I also volunteered some small myrtlewood salmon mementos to accompany the guests when they returned to their faraway homeland, and Phil readily accepted the gifts with the personal touch.

Wine, food, and refreshments abounded, and the guests from afar were well entertained by the offerings of the region. Since the growing of lavender is one of Shobu's specialties, sprigs of the aromatic herb were passed around by our Japanese visitors, and the fragrance wafted through the air. Both Phils were personable and accommodating by nature and, with twinkling eyes and generous hosting, they purveyed over the afternoon event, which went off without a hitch.

I was impressed by one of the Japanese guest's knowledge of our Wild West culture, who informed me of the popularity of log cabins and rustic woods in his country. As we talked, the man's eyes shifted continually to admire a howling wolf I had carved with the look of rustic cliffs blended into the piece. When I offered to ship it to his home, the deal was done, and he happily became the new owner of a rustic piece of our western culture.

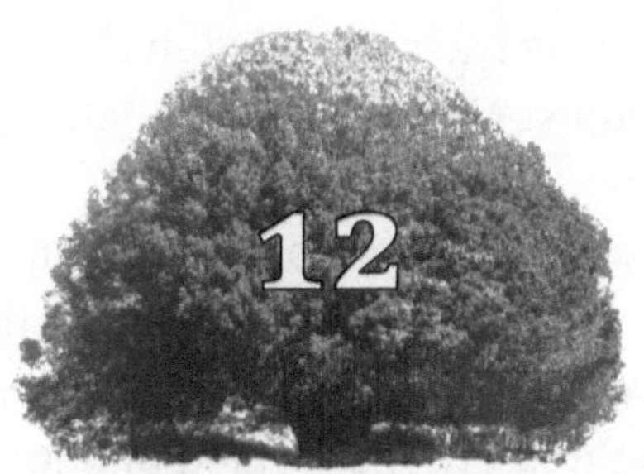

12

The Nature of It All

If the redwood is the granddaddy of trees (the tallest on earth) then myrtles, growing in the same environment, could be called the delicate li'l sister, blushing away along the creeks and in the understory of the sky bound conifers. On the heels of the first "Save the Redwoods League" that built momentum in Northern California, a "Save the Myrtle Wood League" sprouted up in Oregon. The newer Oregon venture mirrored California's early 20th-Century conservation attempts that garnered national attention due to the state's majestic redwood trees. The highly esteemed state forester and conservationist Thornton T. Munger helped establish the Save the Myrtle Wood League that was a precursor of the Save the Myrtle Woods, Inc. and early on served as its president.

Li'l Sister Myrtle was rare enough and precious enough that the Garden Club of America and other organized civic groups began lobbying to protect many groves of this tree still standing. After decades of extensive clearing of myrtle habitat for farmland and myrtle factory uses, the rapid disappearance of the tree and need for preservation became apparent. This new appreciation of myrtlewood and the campaign for these trees emerged in the 1940s, with Portland philanthropist Maria C. Jackson taking the reins as its main supporter.

Maria Jackson, the wife of Portland newspaper baron Charles Samuel Jackson, found herself on this campaign in an era of renewal, a rediscovery of Oregon's impressive landscapes. Foresighted groups formed and lobbied to protect and maintain the untold natural beauty revealed alongside the many new roads of the time, including those in myrtlewood country. When highways began interconnecting miles of mountains, forest lands, and coastlines with populated interior valleys, our wild nature came sharply into focus and an outcry developed for wilderness preservation well before modern day environmental concerns.

On one particular mission, Jackson and company ventured deep into the Coast Range mountains on gravel roads far from the security of their home cities to the north. Even the comfortable limousine could not keep the rocks from pelting the undercarriage and the rising dust clouds from indiscriminately shrouding the long trek. Luckily, Jackson had a loyal and reliable chauffeur at the helm who managed the miles undaunted (a notable fact since his service was later rewarded in Jackson's willed estate).

In 1946, Save the Myrtle Woods, Inc. purchased 42 acres on Brummit Creek's east fork near the small isolated hamlet of Sitkum. The Jackson caravan targeted this destination, a pristine grove of old growth myrtle trees, some measuring 11' across, that inhabited a flat of rich bottomland buried under large ferns. The moss-draped trees sported numerous burl out-growths and intertwined tree formations created by eons of undisturbed augmentation.

Once the motorcade had emptied out and assessed the grove, the ceremony began and a bronze plaque set on a large stone was acknowledged as Jackson reveled in her "mission accomplished" moment. The plaque stated their intent with the inscription, "Dedicated to Preserving In Its Natural Condition A Virgin Forest of Oregon Myrtle Trees, a Gift of Mrs. C. S. Jackson to the People of Oregon Through Save the Myrtle Woods, Inc." In 1950 the site became "Maria C. Jackson State Park" after being deeded to the state park system.

The spirited Save the Myrtlewoods campaign also purchased and preserved a scattering of other myrtle lands, including trees lining the Umpqua River east of Reedsport, and the Coquille Myrtle Grove State Natural Site on the banks of the South Fork Coquille River near Powers. Most of the sponsorships arose from the Portland and Salem areas. Millicoma Myrtle Grove State Park along the Millicoma River east of Coos Bay became the park it is today from myrtlewood purchase and preserve programs, and Alfred A. Loeb State Park on the Chetco River east of Brookings became a state park the same way.

If the Maria C. Jackson site is a sprawling, ancient forest of myrtles spread out over 42 acres, the Hoffman Memorial Myrtle Grove is a mega tree sanctuary confined to a postage stamp-sized acreage closer to four acres. Both were brought into a new, up-to-date focus.

Within a few years after the final myrtlewood festival and the temporary Myrtlewood Association reunifica-tions, a hangover of ideas and insights sparked yet another new project. The big idea came slowly at first, a gradual connecting of dots, until the passion that grew turned it into a runaway freight train of immediate objectives

One idea led to another. After I had produced the "In Nature" segment of the stroll down myrtlewood lane in the Festival of the Myrtle Tree, I realized the merits of further bringing our special trees in wild nature into people's reach. Evidence suggested that patrons of myrtlewood shops were not only curious about the wood, but also wanted to know where it came from. The common query, "Were can we see the myrtle trees?" echoed over and over again at the counters of myrtlewood shops.

Redwood groves are conveniently lined up along the coast highway in Northern California, and you'd have to be in a self-driving car with a sack over your head to miss them. The myrtle parks of Oregon, however, are scattered about well away from the main tourism highway on the coast, and it takes some extra effort to find them. Why not encourage that effort and assist in the search for these other evergreen treasures?

Shortly after brainstorming these ideas, I found myself across the desk of the Oregon State Parks district manager who oversaw all of Southern Oregon's state park system. For maximum credibility, I introduced myself as representing the Myrtlewood Association and the Wood Products Co-op of Southern Oregon, of which I was also an active member, and described my Pacific Carvings business. The manager turned out to be casual and easy to talk to, and I'm sure he sensed my enthusiasm about discovering prime stands of myrtle in the park system.

I had a convincing summary of my proposal and gave a thorough list of public sites worthy of people's interest in myrtlewood to the parks manager. Since it served the public, the framing of the project dictated that only public sites were eligible for consideration. Most of these were in parks, but not all. Because of its grandeur and its more accessible central location, the papers pointed to Hoffman Wayside as critical to the program for a planned interpretive grove.

After the parks department head skimmed through the proposals, he looked up from my papers and zeroed in on Hoffman Wayside. "Well, the problem here is, we plan on putting this land up for sale and removing it from our parklands roster."

"You're going to pull the plug on the whole park!" I exclaimed in disbelief, devastated that all the time and thought I'd invested into anchoring the project with this one important grove might be lost. The ultimate blow was losing protection of Hoffman grove.

"Unfortunately, yes," he went on. "It's turned into a liability that we need to downsize." With some hesitation, and seeing my baffled expression, he added, "Let me review your proposals and re-evaluate Hoffman Wayside, and we'll see if we can work with you on this, although it may be too late."

Grasping the thread of hope that he dangled before me, I left the state parks office with the promise of another appointment. It seemed strangely coincidental that the Hoffman site was on the chopping block right when the myrtle grove project had gelled around that one particular park.

Before our next meeting time, I had compiled a detailed approach towards revitalizing Hoffman Wayside and keeping this valuable grove in a state of preservation. I planned to emphasize it as an important interpretive stand of myrtle trees key to anchoring the region-wide project proposal. From studying the grove, I described a dozen natural history features of the ancient giants, including a bee colony humming in a hollow trunk. In my more detailed proposal, a field guide handout would list such features for the visitor to aid in identifying and understanding the unusual growth patterns expressed by the myrtles.

When I returned for our next appointed meeting, I had all my ammunition ready for saving the Hoffman grove. Amazingly, it turned out I didn't need it. The district manager greeted me with a smile and an affirmative for retaining possession of Hoffman Wayside, mainly for the purpose of the interpretive grove that I had suggested. He indicated that the department was fully behind the entire myrtle grove project. I was elated, hardly able to maintain my composure. Gaining a green light from major bureaucracies wasn't supposed to be this straightforward.

Since Hoffman Wayside was already on the table for change, the district manager agreed to reinvent it as a key myrtle stand in the new "Visit the Groves" itinerary. I suggested adding myrtlewood to the name to fit the new focus, like "Hoffman Myrtlewood Wayside," and he countered with "Hoffman Memorial Myrtle Grove." At that point, he handed me off to an interpretive coordinator named Shirley Stentz, who helped me move the project forward.

As the myrtle grove introspective unfolded with Shirley's help, Oregon State Parks pulled all stops. They installed a new sign with the updated Hoffman name and produced the signs at their wooden sign shop for all the groves in the entire project, even parks not under their jurisdiction. Signs at the groves of interest were essential, and would coordinate with the planned brochure of mapped itineraries and explanations. This was the gist of the project, acknowledging groves of interest with an easy-to-read map as a guide. The goals included sparking visitor interest in Oregon's myrtlewood parks and businesses, and giving them a fulfilling nature experience in return, one of tantalizing walks among the sylvan souls.

The first thing I had pursued in generating the region-wide project was to obtain commitments from the people in charge of public lands that fit the plan. Once I had gained a footing with the Oregon State Parks department, I took the lid off the grand plan and encouraged all the myrtlewood people to run with it. This hinged on a Catch-22, since I wanted to avoid promoting any false hopes with premature gestures that might be nixed later. Everything moved forward as planned, however. I met with little or no skepticism, and it was a win-win that fed a promotional circle for all those on board, both parks and myrtlewood shops.

The future of the project looked bright and open-ended, but even more work lay ahead. I contacted the directors of Coos and Douglas county parks, Bureau of Land Management and U.S. Forest Service personnel, various road departments, and all the myrtlewood people that I knew. We developed steering committees, applications for grants were submitted, and soon the project took on a life of its own. Sponsorship came from as far away as the World Forestry Center in Portland, Oregon.

I garnered enthusiasm that translated into an incredible amount of support, engendering many spinoffs of the main plan. For example, the U.S. Forest Service in Gold Beach requested and paid for an actual sign made of myrtlewood that described the world's largest myrtle tree. Clear plastic weatherproofing encased the sign placed near the tree, which grew in their ranger district. Of course this location landed top billing on the Myrtlewood Country brochure coverage, pointing out the tree's circumference of 503", or 13'–6" in diameter.

I also relied on the collected history of the aforementioned preserves established in the 1940s, and compared the old plots with the modern day parks. Part of my plan was to respect those efforts made in the past and add extra visibility to highlight their importance. Since they were purchased for protection as preserves at the beginning, I continued using the term preserve in all references with the hope that they would be honored as such. Some of these myrtle stands were not in parks, but simply bordered the highways of yesteryear, and had been all but forgotten by the road departments. They were all fine groves with easy highway access, especially the Umpqua River route, and were listed in the brochure with designated signage at the sites.

The Myrtlewood Association chased a new purpose once again with meetings held to help coordinate the Myrtlewood Country plan. It was decided all groves would have a small sign with a myrtle tree logo engraved and painted alongside "Myrtlewood Grove Area" with the next line reading "Oregon Myrtlewood Association." The title "Designated Grove of Interest" went with the more explanatory signs posted at a half dozen sites of extra significance.

Alluding once more to redwoods lining the coast highway in Northern California, and in comparison, only one substantial myrtle tree area proliferates in a public park bordering the same coastal highway in Oregon. At this site a massive, abrupt mountain named Humbug pushes up almost 2000' to form a bulwark against the sea. Half of this massif wages a war against erosion as the Pacific Ocean waves tear at her cliffs, while Highway 101 detours around the other half in a long semicircle to rejoin the coastline. Where the highway leaves the sea on the north side of the mountain is where the proliferation of myrtle begins, and all this is encompassed by Humbug Mountain State Park.

Myrtle trees dominate the lower canyon of Humbug with its many hiking trails and line the creek at the official park picnic area. This small meadow scattered with picnic tables and bordered by the evergreen myrtles merited an interpretive sign acknowledging the site as the only myrtle park adjoining the coastal highway. It is also one of the few places with myrtles growing within easy reach of the ocean, since the heavy salt air keeps most of the arboreal world at bay.

An on-the-ground assessment and list of all potential sites in Myrtlewood Country was an immediate priority. I already had an overview of where the noteworthy groves were to be found, and I had visited most locations in the past. But this venture entailed a much more thorough analysis, and as I expanded the search into little known territories with new discoveries, many surprises popped up along the way.

I found myself scouting out a remote section of the Umpqua River, off on a gravel road, to explore a potential addition to Myrtlewood Country. Greenery of steep forested slopes boxed in the river, and reflected off the equally green spread of water. A fleet of merganser ducks suddenly appeared from behind a bend in the wide river, barely skimming the water at break neck speed. In a dramatic appearance, a bald eagle swooped around the same bend, explaining the velocity of the fleeing ducks. When the challenged and the challenger disappeared up river in a fleeting moment, I continued on with my mission. Within a short distance and at a feasible stretch of shoulder upstream from my target, I pulled over and commenced to launch a kayak from the steep bank.

As I paddled along downstream, a thick stand of impressive myrtle trees emerged from a sandy river loam that rose well above the frothing water level. In a few hundred feet the grove ended as the currents cut around on the other side of the trees as well. This was an island, straddling the river as it swept around both sides with equal wave action.

I beached my watercraft and thoroughly explored the features of this well-watered mini-forest of myrtle that dominated the island. I had come to recognize hints of group personalities unique to individual collectives of the myrtle, and I looked for key features in this temperate island jungle. There appeared to be a propensity of natural loop grafts from trunks and branches crossing each other, locking together with inter-growing cells, and silt from continuous flooding coated the tree trunks to waist height.

After checking out both sides of the split waterway, I paddled back to the gravel road with the satisfaction of a noteworthy discovery. What a standout a "Myrtlewood Island" would be in the lineup of groves!

Many miles upriver from the myrtle island, where the north and south forks of this mighty river joined forces to form the main stem Umpqua, a cluster of impressive myrtles held sway at the very inside apex. Since this point was part of Douglas County's Singleton Park, I enlisted this power spot between two rivers as a point of interest on the myrtle grove trail.

As I sought out interesting trees and analyzed different myrtle stands, I began to see more overall characteristics varying from place to place. For example, a collection of myrtles growing on a solid rock shelf reflected their struggle to grow in their shapes and formations. Micro-environments have a direct impact on individual groves, from extra scarring throughout left by rodent gnawing to hollowing of trunks from excess conks and decay. Trees growing on steep north-facing slopes shaded by tall conifers have very limited growth potential that shows in the rings of their wood. I have counted 50 years in 1" of growth from wood specimens in my shop.

A few outstanding myrtle forests lie within easy reach of coastal Highway 101, two on highways linking 101 with the interior valleys of Western Oregon. Thick myrtle preserves are prevalent both east and west of Scottsburg County Park, which edges the Umpqua Rivers 16 miles east of 101 on Highway 38. The Hoffman interpretive grove is 23 miles east of 101 on Highway 42.

Further to the south, two non-connector paved roads boast impressive myrtle groves. Eight miles upriver from Gold Beach, which straddles Highway 101, the Myrtlewood Trail can be found near Lobster Creek. This marked trail on U.S. Forest Service land leads to the largest known myrtle tree. Farther up the Rogue River at Quosatana Campground, magnificent Oregon myrtle stands and specimens make up what some call the "mother of all groves." Alfred A. Loeb State Park, 10 miles up the Chetco River from 101 and the town of Brookings, contains stately myrtles and nearby redwood trees that embody the northern most spread of redwood habitat, all near the state line with California.

An essential element of identifying groves is signage, and the uniform brown wood signs with yellow-painted lettering designated all the groves of interest on the Myrtle-wood Country itinerary with a subtle natural appeal that upgraded the project. The stylized Myrtlewood Association logo resembled a clover leaf of green with a dark tree trunk. I joined the Oregon State Parks sign makers at a barn facility one afternoon to paint the logos after they were engraved.

While I painted the simple but effective myrtle tree logo engraved on each sign, a parks overseer named Don Howard commented, "You're sure lucky you got this going in the off-season of early spring. In the busy summer tourist season ahead this woulda never happened!"

I knew he was right. "I'm extra busy producing carvings all summer long as well," I said, "so I wouldn't be doing this either. This is the small window of opportunity I can devote to this project."

"You know, some of these signs may not last," he added "There's more than bullet holes to worry about." He went on to explain how local vandalism often caused considerable damage to road and park signs. "They cut off posts just for firewood," he explained. "Once we formed some posts in concrete the same size as the common 4" x 4" wood post and painted them to look like wood."

Don had my full attention now. "Sure enough," he said chuckling, "we found chainsaw gouges at the base of the posts! We got some good revenge on that thief, and somebody sure got a torn-up saw chain."

There were obviously more challenges to this project then I'd ever imagined.

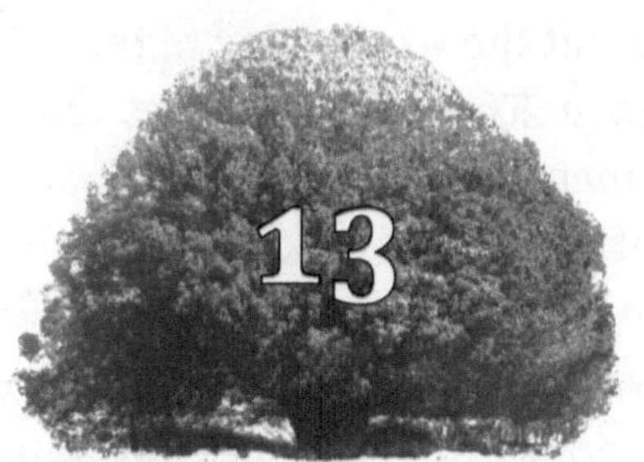

13

Waves of Grain

On another balmy October day, this time in 1993, a team with a common purpose descended upon the Hoffman grove to help welcome all comers to the widely spread plots of these national treasure trees. This one called out for some renovations with its picnic tables in disrepair and overgrown brambles camouflaging the impressive surroundings.

A single stone monolith standing waist high served as the focal point in the shaded flat above the river. A bronze plaque attached to this stone proclaimed the site's heritage and inspired the day's activities led by volunteers from the Myrtlewood Association.

Sharon Mast, aka "Myrtle Gal," and co-owner of the Myrtlewood Gallery with her husband Garreth, tackled the park cleanup with her two young sons. Sharon, who propagated myrtle starts from seed and offered saplings to the public at the gallery, was right at home in the wooded setting. Her potted myrtle plants remain one of the few sources available in the state.

Park personnel helped direct the operation and tended to the mowing of the grassy plots. My wife and youngest daughter joined me along with a handful of other volunteers to round out the work party in the effort to embellish the myrtle grove. The ambiance was casual and friendly, and a picnic lunch lightened the work load and contributed to the pleasant social mix.

We trimmed the overgrown sprouts hiding the myrtles' stalwart foundations to reveal intriguing wood formations. It took many hours to chop back the ferocious tangle of blackberry vines that waged war against us and to haul away the debris of fallen branches.

As visibility improved, we found meandering paths easily followed winding through clusters of trees. Our next step for the interpretive grove was to identify and label any outstanding characteristics of these ancient giants on small metallic plates (with corresponding numbers in the walking guide) to place at the base of the trees. The walking tour guide listed the numbers, along with an explanation of that particular natural history feature, and these hand-outs became available in a drop box attached to a park sign post. A dozen different listings covered the features of these rambling giants, including a variety of burl formations, rodent and bird scarring, and the age and size of the largest tree of the grove.

In the region-wide Myrtlewood Country brochure, many of these features were again described in conjunction with the resultant grain patterns observed in wood cross sections. Photos of wood samples and drawings demonstrated the connection between tree growth and the great variety of myrtlewood grain. Between field work, signage, and brochures, we had the project well established and ready for the public to enjoy informative experiences and appreciate their national treasure tree.

The brochure was widely distributed in myrtlewood shops, visitor centers, and parks departments, and after many reprints, still continues to be in circulation. We were proud to give much-deserved credit in the brochure to all of the parks and businesses whose assistance made this venture possible.

After the long-setting sun of summer gave way to nightfall's darkening shadows, the campers began to trickle in. Although electric spot lights had replaced the traditional campfire at this outdoor amphitheater with its scheduled "campfire talks," the mood of the evening was undaunted and a perfect environment to begin my presentation on Myrtlewood Country. Stoking the air of mystery and intrigue in the atmosphere, I handed out the brochures, serving as guides for the natural history I shared, and encouraged all comers to peer into the eye slots of the shadow box on display.

Inside the large, rectangular box, a 14" tall myrtlewood owl stared back at the viewers with glowing eyes and streaks of light scattering across its carved surfaces. Ultra violet rays from a black light installed inside the box fully illuminated the bird and its significant grain colorations, perfectly demonstrating how myrtlewood is one of the very few phosphorescent woods in the world. As the refraction of light only works on raw wood surfaces, I had not applied any finishes to the owl, thus preserving its luminescent qualities.

From there the talk moved to an Oregon rain forest banana slug that had gardeners in the audience shaking their heads. But even lowly slugs are an iconic part of the ecosystem, and I shared how I'd cut a special piece of myrtlewood with perfect black-and-yellow markings to replicate just such a creature. It was a prime example to show how the coloring in myrtlewood can imitate animals. I also described how the slugs at their slimy best could be found oozing their way up the windows of my forest home until they appeared to be some weird creature of the deep as viewed through a submarine's window.

Then, with a flourish, I announced that the lucky person who found the drawing of a banana slug on their brochure was the winner of the program's door prize. After a buzz of activity and many flashing smiles, the recipient came forward and eagerly accepted her carved banana slug souvenir.

Next, we moved on to explore samples of four distinct types of burl formations: first, the common bird's eye burls that cluster around the base of many myrtlewood trees and sometimes up their trunks and, second, small, spherical nodes that emerge from the burling at the base.

"Marble burl" is an apt description of these nodes, although the revered wood craftsman George Nakishima of Bucks County, Pennsylvania, called them "grape burls," perhaps for their tendency to grow in clusters. These names aside, each single one can be pried from the bark of the "mother burl" at the tree's base. After peeling away the bark from the individual spheres, the pure white wood under-neath can be polished into a genuine myrtlewood "pearl."

The remaining two burls are the smooth, rounded lobes that can grow into enormous sizes, sometimes high up the tree trunks, and a rumpled and variegated-looking lobe that I call a "cauliflower burl."

Among the many natural history props on display for the campfire group sat some of my latest art pieces, including a swooping free-form eagle and a salmon emerging from natural formations. A fully carved 10" x 12" bull elk and a bear grabbing a salmon rounded out the nature-themed selections of myrtlewood art.

We analyzed natural history samples from salvaged tree sections that were hammered by constant pecking of woodpeckers and sap suckers. These cross sections of wood clearly showed a pattern of pecked markings deep in the interior grain patterns after the tree had grown over its wounds. In a distinct interaction of nature, the birds had added their signatures to the figure in the myrtlewood grain.

Gnawing wood rats had created unusual forms on the exterior wood of the myrtles. This aggressive activity usually leaves a circle or oblong patch on the tree where the scar tissue builds up a wrinkled and distorted framing around the wound. I explained how I'd slice many of these patches off large fallen limbs, trim them, and sand the indentations smooth for the application of black-painted lettering to make rustic labels for pieces in many of my art exhibits.

Other samples that I shared included cross-sections of the many colors and grain patterns that this tree's varied wood can host, including a rare soft-pink heartwood. These samples matched photos of the same that were printed in the Myrtlewood Country brochure handed out at this event.

Another mystery tour led the audience into the tree's own world of expression. For over 30 years I had set aside distinct images that appeared in the grain of the wood that I worked. Since these images were from a living entity, they brought the myrtle to a new metaphysical level of self-expression. Of course, there are many variables to consider, but the results revealed in these approximately 3" x 3" cross sections were astounding.

I invited participants to ponder slices of finely sanded wood with uncanny resemblances to birds, animals, and human faces "drawn" by the myrtle's own pigmentations. Most of the best images came from spalted wood, where heavy ink lines induced by bacteria and moisture run rampart through the wood. I had photographed and enlarged the more striking images to make sizable prints on canvas and archival paper for wall hung art. Some of these were digitally color-enhanced for effect; others were left in natural wood colors.

This art concept has been termed *hidden figure design*. Interestingly, seeing things in clouds or in anything else has more recently been labeled *pariedolia*, from the Greek *para* ("beside, alongside, instead of") and the noun *eidolon* ("image, form, shape").

On that note, I wrapped up the state park-sponsored campfire presentation. After the barrage of questions from the group about this previously little-known realm of trees, I felt satisfied knowing I had shared my profound understanding that myrtle trees have many things to express if we choose to spend the time to interpret them. By inviting the audience to take a closer look at my wood artifacts, I cordially extended the evening until the last lingering, conversational campers drifted away.

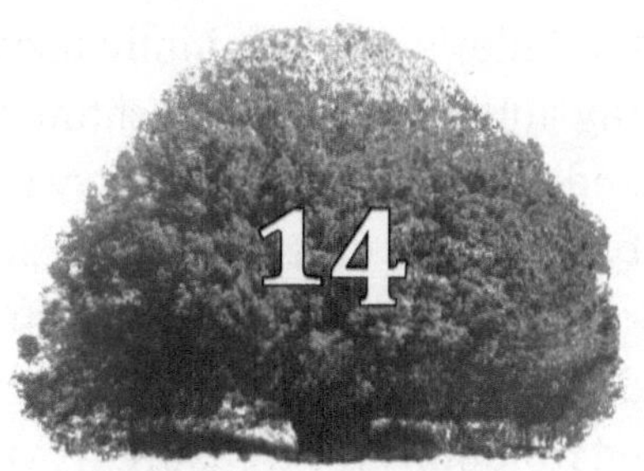

14

Forest Gold

The Weyerhauser timber empire owned 200,000 acres of the southern coast range mountains east of Coos Bay and, as such, also oversaw a prime source of myrtlewood. Aside from their routine cycles of harvesting fir trees, a fellow from New England named Stuart Stein built an internal company program that offered minor forest products to the public in a permitting process. Stuart and I met, and he welcomed my request to salvage old and downed myrtle logs and stumps from the numerous abandoned logging sites on their timber lands.

Together with Lloyd, who already had a permit for minor wood products, we organized forays into the interior of the mountains, and Stuart sent us on our way. Lloyd followed the map he kept in his head, the one created from years of exploring these same mountains that were easily accessed from his home in the foothills, and I followed Lloyd. As we winged along on backwoods gravel, he drove with his inseparable beagle either lying content on his lap or whiffing the air outside the driver-side window.

My Jeep pickup served me well with its 8,000-pound capacity winch and 120' of cable, and carried along an extra 150' of cable, snatch blocks, and a peavey for log rolling. An old oversized faller's saw originally used by the Weyerhauser Company and a modest Stihl chainsaw rounded out everything I needed for tackling the heavy myrtle remnants. I towed a utility trailer for extensive harvesting, but in most cases the pickup bed proved adequate for the amount of wood I needed to handle.

We scouted randomly for treasure troves of abandoned myrtlewood like squirrels gathering cones for the winter, only some of our "cones" were the size of a dishwasher. Using winch lines and cables, we pulled whole logs out of ravines and off hillsides, salvaging only the choicest logs covered with burls or streaked inside with wild colorations. My interests were twofold: logs for cutting dimensional carving stock, and uprooted stumps with their unusual formations conducive to carving abstract wildlife sculptures.

Lloyd had his own objective and searched the hillsides for forest gems. He knew the secrets hidden in the overgrown terrain like no one else and could peel back the layers of 100 years of logging. Even small myrtle trees form clusters of burl wood around the base where the bole meets the roots, and these well-aged stumps of a modest size with a dearth of bark and sap worked well for his craft. Aging cures the wood slowly like a fine wine, deepening and enriching the heartwood into spectacular gold-and-black contrasts that shimmer from the distorted grain found where the tree springs from the earth.

After Lloyd selected a prospective stump, the real labor began. We dug the black earth away from the perimeter and deep into the roots until the stump was clean, followed by cutting away all the roots and undesirable portions. At this point Lloyd set up his compact Alaskan mill frame on top of the stump to which he bolted a small chainsaw that pivoted on the mill frame to make lateral cuts through the stump. The frame, which could be adjusted for the thickness of each slice, stayed uniform as cuts were made.

This is when the magic happens...when the gold of the myrtle shines through, to reveal the core slice of what would someday become a glistening clock gracing the walls of the House of Myrtlewood, and then homes of their purchasers. The unworldly gold-and-black wood grain would leap out when the liquid finishes were applied much later in Lloyd's shop. This was true forest gold, and cutting the clock faces felt like slicing oversized gold nuggets.

Waiting for enough daylight to begin working one early morning, I watched the sunrise crest the ridge tops and evaporate the pockets of mist clinging to the dark green tree lines. Being out in these mountains begat the exhilarating moments that liberate me the most, when a bright sunrise illuminates forested mountains sweeping in all directions and fights back the morning chill. This affinity with the mountains had begun in my youth, when I ran with deer in the hills near home. It was a game I loved to play as a child, stalking upon a small herd until they fled, then running along until they had paused and I caught up to them, sometimes by tracking their hoof prints. There were times I was able to creep up so closely that the deer and I would stare eye-to-eye for minutes at a time.

Today, I was leaning on a steep slope that swung upward in a brush-tangled mass extending beyond sight. I held on for a visual down canyon, anchored in the dark loam that shot ferns up to my chest. The ravine below dropped in a steep angle. In this country, everywhere is steep, and it's said that you're lucky to be born with one leg shorter than the other so you can walk side-hill. Or, as in my case, it's just possible that the lifelong habit of walking side-hill so often causes one leg to stretch out and the other to scrunch up. The results are pretty much the same.

Below me an eroded myrtle stump the size of a refrigerator still wrapped its roots around a one-rock outcrop that towered over my jeep, parked on an overgrown and neglected logging road. Beyond this scene, where the old track fizzled out, I could see the target of my chainsaw; a large burl-encrusted stump sprouted anew with dozens of shoots that sought the sky. Their ambitious growth, however, had been undermined by browsing elk that had cropped them to the ground.

What could be more fitting then to carve a series of bull elk from a bole chawed on by those same animals? My chainsaw found its alignment, made short work of the burled mass, and, after a lengthy process back at the studio, I had my elk series. At their source, the slabs I'd cut to the ground still left plenty of living roots and stump wood to sprout again. With the stubborn will to live inherent in its genes, the future myrtle tree would battle against the elk again and again until it gained a skyward advantage.

To reach this abandoned area, Lloyd and I had followed a system of old grass-covered logging tracks that switch backed and forth below Ivers Peak, stopping occasionally to remove random windfalls that blocked our route. Behind the aforementioned rocky out crop were the remains of three sizable tree wood specimens, one encrusted with burls along its full length. A shallow ravine on the down-hill side of the track also harbored some interesting myrtle logs, one of them a buckskin log, almost always rich in color tones. My chainsaw mill and I got to work, ensuring a second life for the wood in the homes of many.

On a different spot high above the logging spur, another treasure appeared. I had surveyed the entire area for raw materials and stumbled upon a complete uprooted stump swelled with burls. Well beyond the reach of our cables, it was necessary to roll and maneuver it down the steep mountainside with a peavey. This bole with roots flagging off its sides pushed the limits of my endurance, but gravity worked with me as I dodged the thick re-prod fir until the cables were within reach. After this massive effort of retrieval, I was determined to create a one-piece marvel from the contours of the complete burl-stump conglomeration. Ten years later, the completed piece, carved into a life-size seal, was highlighted in a world-class Vancouver, B.C. wildlife art exhibition.

As we cruised way up the Coos River's gravel roads on yet another one of these tree wood searches, Lloyd suddenly pulled over and skidded to a stop without warning. I pulled up behind his vehicle on the road edge and jumped out, thinking maybe something was in the way. "What's up?"

He was clearly agitated, in a state unlike his usual self. "I lost my hand gun, its missing!" he exclaimed, panicked. I looked in through his open window as he frantically searched under and behind his pickup's bench seat while his trusty beagle cowered in its far corner. Lloyd seemed more engulfed in this emergency then a misplaced weapon would merit, especially when there was no need for it at the time.

"You probably left it at your house," I said, trying to talk him down, but he remained inconsolable. Perplexed, I watched as he spun his truck around and roared back homeward, our mission obviously aborted.

Why was he so distraught over a minor problem? I wondered. Then it dawned on me. Lloyd required the security of his hand gun around the clock. Though cheerful and friendly, an unseen dark shadow hung over him like a veil. Even though it had happened 10 years before we'd met, he had once recounted his loss to me.

The tragedy had played out at La Verne County Park on an idling summer day, a long, hot, and unforgiving day, when two teenage girls were accosted by an unstable young man. Although the unfolding of events still remained sketchy, the 23-year-old evildoer had shot both young girls dead, one of them Lloyd's daughter.

Postponing our myrtlewood quest for another day now seemed a small sacrifice to make and, turning around, I drove out of the mountains and homeward.

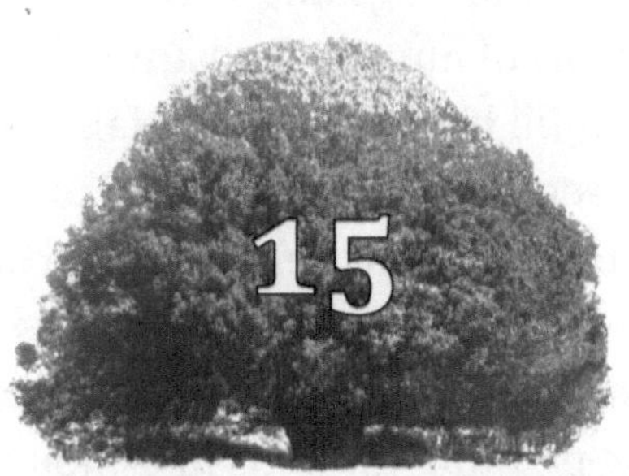

15

Gold of the Heart

Myrtle gold merged with the real thing in the earliest days of my myrtlewood quests. Near the end of a gravel road, letters cut from rustic wood proclaimed the residence of "Jack and Jill," and yes, they lived up the hill—Hoover Hill to be exact, but more importantly, their quaint log cabin nestled alongside Ollala Creek. About 100 million years ago, when volcanic islands from somewhere around the equator slammed into western North America, they brought gold deposits that trickled into many waterways, including, much to Jack and Jill's good fortune, Ollala Creek.

On the threshold of the 1970s, celebrations of art, music, and wine sprinkled with a universal incense blossomed everywhere, and I was not alone in being swept along, more as a participant than observer. One event brainstormed by a local commune was a spring arts and craft fair, which was to be forever known as the "Spring Fair." It was at this event that I first exhibited artworks gleaned from infatuations with myrtlewood and the observation of wildlife while working at a wild game park. It was there that I had the opportunity to follow my chosen path by presenting a display of wildlife carvings and rustic wood shapes turned into various forms of humans and animals.

As Jack and Jill browsed the art fair held at the county fairgrounds, it seemed Jack was drawn to my works, and to one piece in particular. This very hard myrtlewood segment of burl grain was one that I had labored over for many hours, using only hand chisels and gouges to relief carve an old prospector panning for gold in a mountain stream. I'd acquired this unique chunk of stump wood with a borrowed chainsaw, the only power tool I'd used.

Jack came and went, and mused over this piece for quite some time, and finally introduced himself. "I would like to add some small nuggets to your carving and give the carved miner his prize," he said, surprising me with his proposal. I thanked him graciously, overwhelmed by this gentleman's generosity toward my work.

Sure enough, Jack returned to the art show the following day with a vial of gold flecks and three small nuggets, proclaiming, "I panned these myself, out of our creek," and went on to explain where he lived and some of his pursuits in life. We discussed the placement of the nuggets in the carving, and it all fit together well. Although this relief carving was rather crudely done in the early and humble beginnings of my artistic pursuits, this kind and wizardly elder seemed happy to reward my unbridled enthusiasm to create art with a generous contribution to the carving.

Since that time, the gold miner piece, in all its rugged and rustic glory, has transformed into a talisman, a symbolic witness and reminder for the tenacity needed to maintain a career as a nature artist with a medium of hardwood.

Perhaps this soul secret sounds quirky, but this talisman has remained a pivotal inspiration throughout my art career, both a study and reinforcement of my convictions.

I had determined early on that myrtlewood engendered my potential wealth in life, and this piece epitomized that ideal perfectly. Gold nuggets added to the carving expressed the concept that myrtlewood, along with hard work, generated the "gold" of my career.

At art exhibitions over the years I am often asked, "Do you keep any of your own work?" and "You must have some nice work in your home." The answer is always the same; the art I create must go out into the world because part of the challenge of creating my sculptures is to ensure that they will be desired by others. I do not cling to even the most impressive of pieces, or any random sculpture creation demanding a piece of my heart and soul. Only one exception stands alone in my possession; a rustic myrtlewood slab carved into a grizzled old prospector hitting pay dirt in a stream, with two small nuggets and gold dust sprinkled in his pan, and a nugget held out between his thumb and forefinger for all to see.

When the nuggets were set in place on the carved gold panning scene, the piece caught the admiring eye of a stalwart companion of my childhood. In the neighborhood realm of our youth, Dave was anointed "Dude" in a game of juvenile nomenclature, mostly instigated by his older brother, aka "Buzzard Bait." Mind you, this was eons before the mainstream cliché "Dude" came into vogue, and when we watched the father of Jeff (the Dude) Bridges play scuba hero on the television show *Sea Hunt.*

Dude and his brother became caught up in a quest for gold, which aligned with a penchant for gambling. With their sharp mathematical minds, the duo took on Reno, Nevada's gaming houses. After their share of successful bouts, the youthful pair were booted for card counting. Alas, too much skill and brain power can get one into trouble. These two seekers of wealth were my first cousins and, throughout my childhood, Dave was more like a brother to me. His swarthy features trickled down from the dark complexion of our grandmother and the wavy dark hair of our grandfather, an Arizona cowboy. I got a touch of wave in my hair and usually tan easily without excessive burning and, at a certain stage of our lives, we both wanted to be cowboys.

In a pensive time of my life, shortly after my own son was born, a phone call begat a new adventure. "Whatduya say we head into the mountains to the south and seek out some placer gold" came the persuasive proposal from my cousin Dave, who was still under the spell of gold fever. Since the suggestion came from my childhood companion of many outdoor adventures and mischief, and with new myrtlewood habitats beckoning, my quick response landed us deep in a Klamath Mountains wilderness by the week's end.

When the gravel road ended we began back packing down a wild river trail, following along the cliff edge above the aqua blue waters that cascaded through the rugged canyon. Panning some of the promising feeder creeks to this remote river was our plan, and we had enough provisions to camp along the way. Early into the hike, sea shell fossils appeared in a rock outcropping, hinting at a time when everything surrounding us was under an ocean.

Despite the intense summer heat the thrill of adventure propelled us forward until I heard what sounded like an angry bee buzzing close to my ear in the shoulder-high brush lining the trail. Instinctively, I dodged away from the brush and the assumed location of the buzzing and found myself a step away from a rattlesnake beginning to coil in the middle of the trail. The all-encompassing sound became louder as an adrenaline rush pushed me backwards and into the Dude.

After the near miss of a rattlesnake strike, we scrutinized the hot dusty trail ahead with its formidable rock cliffs and, looking at each other, decided on plan B. Driving high up to the cooler ridge tops and accessing the same feeder creeks well above the main river sounded like a better plan, so early afternoon found us winding down an old logging road in remote forests thousands of feet above the river canyon we had abandoned.

As we descended a forest road along a gushing mountain spill called Silver Creek, an old mine shack appeared, and as I stopped the vehicle, two guys of our generation approached from the cabin. After some friendly discourse on life in the hills and gold mining, they informed us that most of Silver Creek was staked with claims.

"Why don't you guys work part of our stretch of Silver Creek for some nuggets," one of the claim holders named Moses asked. "You'll be doing us a favor by clearing off the over burden." He further explained that more gold would wash down with each winter runoff and the cleared section of creek bed would trap future deposits of the mineral for them, a win-win for everyone.

We readily agreed to the task, and as the late afternoon heat lazily subsided, Moses guided us a quarter mile upstream where we set up camp and, after lining out the next day's goals for us, he melted back into the forest. Starting at first dawn, Dave and I removed all the over-burden down to bed rock from a section of the creek, working the gravel in a sluice box as we went and, before noon, were rewarded with one fine yellow nugget the size of a man's fingernail.

Since we tend to look up when in need of clarity, as if seeking messages from the heavens, I held the small yellow stone above my head, tempting the rays of bright sunlight as they bent their way through the dense conifer forest. Finally a bright glint appeared on the gold, illuminating a mesmerizing shape, the unmistakable image of a wolf's head. Although supposedly absent from these mountains for many years, I could still imagine the cry of the lone wolf resonating in the tree tops and echoed by the nugget.

Even as I observe the many expressions coming from the wood of myrtle trees, I found the same forest spirits at work in the soft glint of mineral, and I nudged Dave to share the newly found image. Moses appeared seemingly from out of nowhere, as he always did, and congratulated us on our find. He proudly clarified that the Silver Creek gold has been assayed and contains fewer of the impurities normally found in gold, thus the rich yellow hue of our nugget.

After pulling more bits of gold from cracks in the bedrock and panning for sprinkles of the metal, we ventured further afield. The following morning found us a few miles downstream at the trailhead of a noteworthy waterfall that rushed Silver Creek along on its journey to the sea. Access to the falls required edging along a sheer, sliding gravel drop-off on a trail cut no more than a foot wide, hundreds of feet above the creek.

What seemed like an extreme canyon of a lost world opened up beneath the trail. Huge old growth Port Orford cedar trees, a rare and monumentally beautiful species of white cedar, dotted the canyon floor while mountains formed of single rocks towered above. After winding down to the bottom we worked our way back up Silver Creek until the rock walls closed in on three sides and the creek poured over the top precipice in a thundering fall 150 feet above our heads. We ambled over, under, around, and through the maze of truck-sized boulders and narrow tunnels in the final approach to the showering blast of the waterfall. We could only imagine the amount of gold trapped under the immovable stone garden at the base of the falls.

As the afternoon waned, a flat shelf beyond the boulders beckoned us to establish camp. In the deepest pools of the cold, foaming overflow of the waterfall, shadows of trout had appeared, and I didn't let this go unnoticed. After pulling out a small fishing pole, I boasted to the Dude, "You'll need to rustle up a fire to cook all the fish I'm gonna catch!"

"You're not going to find any worms in this dry soil, so I'm not getting my hopes up," he said, but when he saw me snapping my pole together with confidence, his curiosity got the best of him. "How you gonna catch those skittish wild trout without bait?" he asked.

"Dude, I'm resource-full," I said, drawing out the words.

"Full of it, alright," Dude bantered back.

It was true I didn't even have a spinner as I set out on a bare-bones mission with only small hooks and a pole. I had looked over the terrain around the pools and surmised that the red, unripened blackberries resembled salmon eggs, a favorite for any salmonid species. Besides, wild, hungry fish are known to strike anything hitting the water.

I rounded off some select berries to a smaller size with a pocket knife, wove one onto the hook, and quietly leaned the pole over a prime pool. The trout were easy to see in the pure, crystalline waters and I dropped the bait in front of one. He immediately lunged at the berry. To my pleasant surprise, my strategy worked and in no time I had half a dozen nice fish.

We had blazed our trail to this remote, magical site and, with the crescendo of Silver Creek Falls behind us, settled in for another night in the outdoors we shared. The campfire coals glowed red-orange as the fish fried on shish kabob sticks disappeared. "I can't believe how you found a way to catch these wild fish," Dude commented.

"Hey, you caught your share at Twin Lakes that time," I said.

"I remember that well. I know we feasted well on trout, but how many fish did we catch that last day?"

"Fourteen! And all on grasshoppers for bait. I'd read about it in a kid's book." We'd had lots of bait and tackle for those wilderness lakes and the two mile hike-in, but nothing had worked until we started catching grasshoppers. When we were at junior-high age, one of our parents would drop us off at the lake's trailhead at the end of a forest road, and the other parents would pick us up four days later.

If I was the innovative dreamer, Dave had always been the steadfast logical one. From childhood on, I always took the lead on our many hikes, mainly because my exuberance couldn't be contained, but Dave held a steady hand on our course. After some further reminiscences, the mood grew quiet with the impending black of night and its blazing stars, and the last coals of the fire were left behind with sleep.

The next day, while hiking back to our gold-panning camp, a great horned owl glided silently through the conifers, deftly dodging their trunks as the bright sunlight filtered through the shadows. It was a fitting last chapter to a fulfilling adventure, and before long we would be leaving this sparkling wilderness behind. But first, there was a long haul back to my vehicle parked at the miner's shack. Besides the camp gear, I had cut some prime myrtlewood and white cedar segments from dead wood along Silver Creek to salvage.

As I gathered up the heavy myrtlewood treasures for the long haul-out, Moses appeared and willingly loaded up his arms and strode out beside us. He knew my wood carving ambitions and, obviously, the gold he methodically sought on his claim had also settled in his heart.

Our hard-earned booty consisted of a vial of gold flakes and specks, and the one magical nugget in the image of a wolf's head. My fair-minded cousin suggested that we flip a coin to divide up the spoils. I won the toss and, with a gold chain attached, the nugget found its place with my wife and mother of our new born son, daughter and daughter-to-be. Dave took his wizardry with math and technology to the Gulf Coast, where he programmed slot machines for the casinos, while I followed my fate to the Oregon Coast.

When the typical long, hot, dry spell of late August encompasses the central Pacific coastline of North America, the transition to clouds and major rain events is never immediate. A gradual overcast build-up of many days normally precedes the actual down pouring of real rain—at least until this day.

It was another bright and sunny morning, one of many in a row, and I mentally planned the work routine as I often do while walking up the hill to the forested wood-shop/studio I'd built where all my artworks begin and end. While approaching the day's project of production carving-for-dollars, I was abruptly distracted to a side project in the works, drawn by an irresistible urge to carve waves and moving water on a whale piece.

Admittedly, I am sometimes distracted from my planned discipline with callings of greater inspiration, but this move seemed of an unusually intense focus. Not an ordinary undertaking, the planned sculpture featured a breaching humpback whale with cliffs in the background and, of course, the ocean swirling beneath. Many months were required to sculpt an entire log section 4' in length and 2' in diameter, dissecting hundreds of pounds of the dense hardwood in the process.

The three-dimensional whale was already released from the core of the tree remnant, and there were many options to pursue; details of the whale, seabirds, the cliffs, trees on the cliff tops, cleanup work all the way around. Yet today I was drawn to the challenge of carving the movement of oceanic water around the whale, and set to the task. Relishing the curves and flows of imaginary wave action, I guided the gouges and grinder bits through the wood surface as the aromatic chips covered the floor.

While caught up in the intensity of creating flowing waves of wood, I hardly noticed the gathering dark clouds. Even with the large bay shop door open I was taken by surprise when a freak downpour of steady rain suddenly hammered the shop roof. Rushing outside in disbelief, I soaked in the heavy, humid air of a summer downpour. At least an hour of steady rain finally dissipated with some last valiant sputters, and by early afternoon the freak storm was over. After this unusual weather event, the skies cleared and returned to the long stretches of blue sky and sunshine.

The main cities of the area are a mere five miles away as the crows fly (and they do, nesting nearby after scavenging those cities) and were unscathed by any precipitation. Only one inland town located over the hills and into the Coast Range recorded rainfall that afternoon and, true to the season, the entire county lavished in many more days devoid of clouds and rain.

It was a strange weather event, but stranger things became clear as time progressed. Two thousand seven hundred miles to the southeast, a monster storm had made an early morning landfall that same day, blasting the shore-line with hurricane winds and drowning the landscape with tsunami surges of the sea. It was August 29, 2005, and the storm's name was Katrina.

I had given little or no thought to the historical hurri-cane until I watched the television news that evening. I discovered destruction beyond belief while watching the camera crews scan the gulf coastline from news helicop-ters. The causeway of the main coastal highway across Bay St. Louis, where the very eye of Katrina landed, was twisted wreckage, and in many places, completely absent. Cameras running nonstop swept to the east end of the causeway and to Pass Christian, the adjoining town that looked like a giant had scattered an endless box of toothpicks along what was once prime coastal habitation—and the home of the Dude.

I could see my cousin's neighborhood on the inland side of the highway, and there seemed to be a scattering of buildings and a few houses still standing back against the tree line. I was comforted by the reassurance that he would have evacuated, as he always had in the past, when hurricanes threatened. Or had he? With the intensity of the storm and its destructive aftermath, I felt uneasy about the slightest possibility that he had stayed behind.

A quick call to his frantic mother verified my worst fear. Dave had not evacuated! He had grown tired of many false alarms over the years when he had evacuated only to find his home unscathed by the many hurricane landings. This time, he was nonchalant about the approaching storm and refused to leave, even though she'd pressed him to evacuate with numerous phone calls.

Thus began a tirade of day-after-day, back-and-forth phone calls for updates and queries, but with no word from Dave. Finally, five days after Katrina hit and on my birthday,

I received the call. "Here's a birthday present for you," was Dad Roy's greeting, "your cousin is alive and well."

It seemed that on the day of Katrina's landfall as the forceful winds swept around him and water began filling his low lying two-story house, Dave knew this was more than the ordinary hurricane. The roof was refuge from the floods, but impossible in face of the wind, which was busy flattening most of the dwellings in his town.

Bivouacked inside his own home without an axe or chainsaw, there was no way out, and he knew he was caught in the clutches of fate as the water slowly and steadily chased him up the stairs and fully engulfed the main floor of the house. The steady onslaught of the surging flood came up to his knees, up to the edge of his bed. At that point, in his own words, "I was ready to take a big gulp of air, and dive down the stairwell," to face his own demise head on.

And then it had stopped. Slowly, and with the same certainty of the water's rise engulfing the house, it had begun to recede. Comforted by the water level's dropping, Dave had fallen on the bed to escape the sheer exhaustion wrought by the monster cyclone that had been busy flinging mortals into oblivion.

Two days later, after the storm surges left only pockets of water and extended marshes, a neighbor returning to check on his house gave Dave a ride to the nearest relief shelter. After two more days, Dave, a software engineer, had finally phoned out when service was restored at his nearby workplace of Long Beach, Mississippi.

During the same uncanny time frame when I was carving oceanic myrtlewood water forms in a freak north-west downpour, my closest cousin was at the mercy of drowning storm surges from the sea.

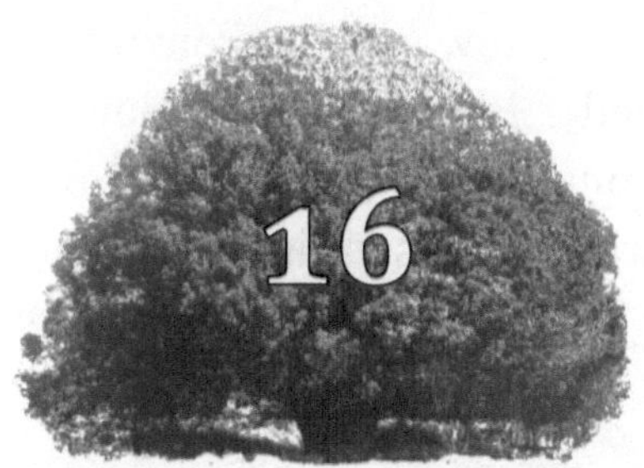

16

Climbing the Tower of Dreams

Twenty or more violins bowing 1,000 notes lifted me across the octagon hall and into a new world, as the crescendo of a Christmas concerto rose and fell in a mighty out pouring of holiday spirit. Young people, they were, intent on their well-synchronized performance of cheer that uplifted everyone at hand and, on this Friday morning, set the mood for the weekend show ahead.

Giddy with the prevailing harmony of violins, I floated down the open aisle between the uptempo musicians, and felt propelled up to a wide wall of window glass, where my vision carried me into extensive Japanese gardens on the other side. This must be a dream, I thought, as a voluminous waterfall pulsated to the stringed instruments as it poured from the center of the rock garden. The glass towering above me permitted an overlay of tree tops and sky to frame the expansive Zen-like nature setting outside.

If my shoes had actually touched the floor, these were my first steps into the World Forestry Center of Portland, Oregon and the debut of my works in a large city. This spot where the glass had stopped me was my assigned booth space destined to bring myrtlewood art to that city. *Unbelievable!*

I turned back toward the frenzied violinists. In that moment, I spied a large, solid myrtlewood table dividing the area with long, elegant file cabinets on each side. These cabinets apparently housed the files related to the history of timber and forestry in Oregon and the thick, substantial table made of my kind of wood served as a station for its research.

I could not have imagined a more fitting atmosphere for showing my work than what surrounded me. Any artist's life is full of setbacks and foiled attempts at success, along with those fleeting moments of grandeur. This was a moment of grandeur. In the old adage of one step forward and three steps back, this, in my career, represented a huge leap forward. Here I was, taking my myrtlewood wildlife carvings out into the world and into the city life of Portland, and doing it in the perfect setting.

As I came and went, setting up my display of myrtlewood carvings, I noticed an open staircase at the side of the hall. A platform jutted out half way up to the second floor balcony of exhibits, where a 3'-long bear carved in dark wood had made himself at home, eyeing the patrons that climbed the steps. His eyes stared over a large fish clamped in his jaws, his challenging look warning all comers, "Don't get any ideas. This is my fish!"

The 100-pound carving with its permanent station in the Forestry Center came from the hands of Masamichi Nitani, of Japanese Ainu descent. Originally from Hokkaido, the island known for its bear carvings by the Ainu people, Nitani brought his wood-carving skills from Japan to Portland where he has resided and worked for many years.

The Western Woodcarvers Association included Nitani and many other talented wood carvers who were exhibiting their work in this annual holiday show. Though I lived and worked far from the Portland metropolis, they had welcomed me into the club and their hosted exhibit, expressing interest in my work with a sense of camaraderie.

My enthusiasm poured forth unabated for the duration of this festive event. I enjoyed constant exchanges with the many patrons, got to know the regulars, and looked forward to repeating the experience in the future from this first step in the early 1980s. Within a few years I became comfortable with this novel holiday routine of the woodcarvers show, which added a new line of income that helped bolster the tourist season drop-off on the south coast.

History shows that Mary Clark (unrelated to B. Roger Clark) was one of the dedicated supporters of Oregon forests and the World Forestry Center. This comes as no surprise as her husband had been an owner-operator of one of our major lumber mills and could be found in those historic forestry center files. With her husband and other close family members on her mind, on a day in early December Mary Clark set off on a pre-holiday jaunt.

Confident that she could find fresh and new offerings at her destination, Clark followed a familiar uphill route all the way to the top until Washington Park unfolded in her line of sight. During the drive to the park, she had sorted through the list implanted on her mental radar, since nothing's quite like the holiday season with that unforgiving deadline putting you on notice.

Comforted by the familiarity of the capacious park, Clark negotiated its entry lane into the Oregon Zoo before her. Beyond the zoo, she knew all too well that the beautiful rose gardens lending acclaim to her City of Roses could be found on a hillside overlooking the city. Though the miles of forested hiking trails that wound throughout and the nearby Japanese gardens were always a temptation, they were bypassed on this wintry day.

Today, Mary Clark had a different mission, her attention focused on the World Forestry Center perched on the hillside overlooking the zoo and host of the Annual Western Woodcarvers Holiday show. She planned to scout the show for the perfect gifts in this season of giving, and, besides, it was an enjoyable, festive time of the year to mix with the crowds at the center.

By the time the crowds were in full swing on that same Saturday afternoon, I had sold a few stocking stuffer-sized carvings and had chatted up some Portlanders I had come to know. One middle-aged fellow, a true art aficionado, stopped by my booth to regale me with his yearly commentary. It was unfortunate that he relied on a cane for getting around, yet he could lean into a conversation with extra comfort.

"You know, I really like your work," he began, "and I know real art when I see it. My sister is an artist, and she was a good friend of Georgia O'Keefe and worked out there in New Mexico."

"Why, that's something to be proud of," I responded. "Thanks for appreciating my work." While we talked, I took note of a stately woman who was studying my North American wildlife series, but when I looked up again, the woman had disappeared.

When I finally paused for a deep breath during the tempo of the busy afternoon, the same woman reappeared, sat down on my booth chair without any hesitation, and pulled out a small notepad and pen. With a commanding air, and flashing a big rock on her ring finger, she began pointing out the art pieces that interested her. She had me scrambling about from one piece to another like a merchant on the ancient Great Silk Road, with my heart racing as if I were running down that same road.

It was Mary Clark, come to check off her Christmas gift list, and she had started at my booth! First, there was the bugling elk, then came the leaping deer suspended over a stump and carved from one piece of banded myrtlewood, followed by the bighorn ram leaning over a cliff edge with its fluted horns proudly raised. "Do you carve these pieces in numbers?" she asked. "Can you carve another of the deer for me?"

I nodded, delighted, and described the method of roughing out these 12" to 14" tall animals from a hand-carved, original model. "It's not that different from bronze sculpture, where an edition of many numbers can be dupli-cated from the same mold based on one original sculpture," I explained. "In both cases there is a substantial amount of finish work that goes into every individual piece."

"Well, in that case," she said, "please make me one more deer carving and ship it to me."

"Certainly," I replied, and proceeded to box up her newly acquired artworks and transported them to her car, thanking her profusely for her interest in my work. Happily, Mary Clark remained an avid collector of my myrtlewood art for many years.

With the evolution of Pacific Carvings and more annual woodcarver holiday shows under my belt, I had built up an advanced inventory of carvings. One particular piece that I showcased regularly at the Forestry Center event was a stylized eagle statuette with wings pointed straight up and head looking down as if seeking prey. This 12"-tall statuette came mounted to a thin, flat base with room to attach a brass nameplate.

In essence, this mini-sculpture served as a special award ordered by, and supplied to, the U.S. National Forest Service. Altogether, four of their offices in different Southern Oregon regions ordered these regularly as a tribute to the dedication of Forest Service personnel, awards given out to acknowledge years of service, often of retirees, and other merits. Due to the Service's obvious link to the Forestry Center, I made a point of keeping one on display whenever I exhibited at the holiday shows.

One year, the USFS headquarters in Washington, D.C. mandated that all awards issued nationwide be their new mass-produced and distributed version: a small, bronzy-looking disc with some generic verbiage and etched design. This was decreed as their one-size-fits-all award for all USFS offices. Needless to say, I was disappointed.

I then received a phone call alert from one of my Forest Service customers who explained the new rules and warned that I might lose all their business. *Might lose their business?* Although they much preferred my 3-D eagle design in the fantastic local myrtlewood and were pushing back against the government bureaucracy and their generic award stipulations, she didn't know what the outcome would be.

As it turned out, I'd worried for nothing. Somehow, they found a way to circumvent the upper authorities and keep my unique eagle renditions in circulation. The orders never stopped and I continued to help them reward their dedicated employees with one-of-a-kind statuettes of Oregon myrtlewood from local forests.

Every artist that exhibits their work in the public eye is familiar with the common queries that come their way.

The number one conversation starter, to which most artists will attest, is, "How long did it take to create this or that piece of art?" My short answer—usually left unspoken—is "a lifetime." With that said, it seems that, in the viewer's eye, time invested somehow equates to the value of the piece. The second most predictable question, confined only to wood artists, is, "Whar duh ya git yer wood?" Again, short answer—the one that I keep to myself—"Wherever I find it." I have pleasantly responded to these same queries with more well-groomed explanations hundreds of times.

People also love to comment on my name, Woodall, seeing as it incorporates my profession. I get comments from, "You sure were born with the right name," to a quizzical, "Is that really your real name?" and, "Your name sure goes along with what you do!" I kid around with them with comments like "It's my Hollywood handle," but the truth is that Woodall is the name I was born with, as were Mr. Woodard and Mr. Woodruff, who also exhibit work with the Western Woodcarvers Association of Portland.

Beads, Bangles & Champagne

From the edge of Coos Bay, I once again made the 100-mile trip north to the town of Newport and to that dominating old building entrenched in Old Town with its bay-side waterfront. I pulled up to the same curb fronting this edifice as I had before, beneath giant block letters painted on a commanding wall announcing "The Wood Gallery," the owner of which had spurned my work years earlier.

My wife Carlin, sitting next to me and excited for the evening ahead, had even bought a new dress for the occasion. It was the opening night of my first gallery show, a month-long exhibition of my work hosted by an art gallery, and the floral design of her dress seemed to match this flowering of our lives.

The clink of toasting champagne glasses could be heard above the soft music that wafted over the gallery, where beauties in beads and bangles mixed with couples coursing through, and with twinkly eyed old gents clinging to each moment. The dance of the hour was a celebration of the visual arts and a nod to three regional artists and their heartfelt expressions.

Romance permeated the air as Kelly, the sponsor of the show and owner of the gallery, had announced his engagement to Cheryl, who had recently came on board as a co-worker. They both commandeered the floor as host and hostess extraordinaire, and ensured the successful opening night of the exhibit, billed as "Original Art in Pure Form." This format acknowledged the artists in the show, and we were all feeling the rush of being in the summer of our professional lives.

For the first time I felt recognized as a visual artist, even though I'd always had utmost confidence in the validity of my works. Convincing the rest of the world of that validity and having it confirmed, however, is an entirely different matter, since you must be blessed by the court of public opinion and remember that the proof is in the purchase.

My mantras beat loudly that night, right alongside my heartbeat. *Be true to who you are and have faith, even blind faith, in the worth of your work.* Many times I coulda, woulda, even maybe shoulda, given up and quit, but I didn't. On a non-stop trajectory against all odds, that Friday night of April 3, 1987 proved it all was meant to be. I had brought myrtlewood to a new level in a theater of fine art. My stained orcas mounted on driftwood waves, including a pod of four on one base, were a featured hit of the show, and backed up by sculptures of humpback whales, seals and sea lions, and a sea otter floating on its back.

I was not alone in this endeavor, but had relied on the help of many. My early associate Bill Leslie, that natural-born salesman, had paved the way for my carvings to be offered from the Wood Gallery's showroom floor, which had eventually led to this special art exhibit. He'd also convinced an art gallery on the island of Kauai, Hawaii to feature my sea life art. Both of these galleries resulted in a long-term turnover of sales and a predictable demand for the myrtlewood sea life compositions of my own creation.

When the commotion had died down and the lights went dim, Carlin and I walked along the dockside amongst the Newport piers in fog-muffled moonlight, where the occasional vagrant sea gulls were making their last run at the seafood scraps from tethered fishing boats. The salt air mixed with the pungent marine life in an intoxicating hint of that crucible of life, the sea with its offspring of creatures. The vessels harnessed to the piers groaned as the tide tugged at their ropes and crab traps stacked here and there on the docks awaited their next plunge into the sea. We were silent, my wife and I, for no words needed to be spoken. The future would keep coming. We were ready for it, and we would meet it head on.

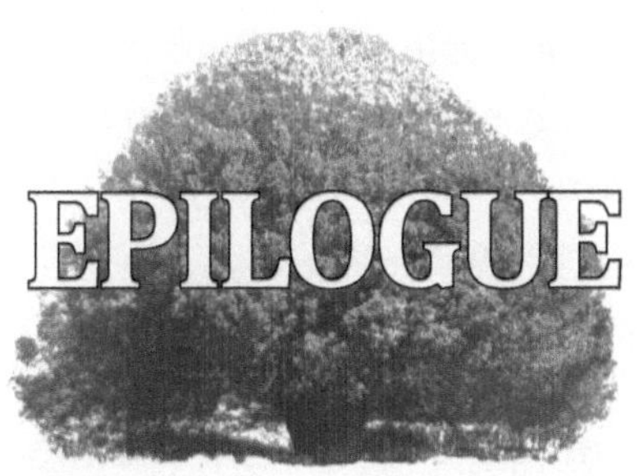

EPILOGUE

The Music Plays On

"Turkey in the Straw, Turkey in the Straw, Pick up your fiddle and rosin your bow, And put on a tune called Turkey in the Straw."

The fiddler picked up momentum, belting out an irresistible toe tapping tune, and wowed the crowd until they were dancing a jig on the spot. But for William Marshall Humbert, this was a side diversion, a simple test for a master violin maker. In his full-blown myrtlewood shop anchored to the east side of Coos Bay, Humbert specialized in these music-making instruments of myrtlewood. This Pied Piper of Eastside built his shop in approximately 1910 and constructed his special violins of fiddle-back myrtlewood with spruce sounding boards through the 1920s.

"I had this world class violinist, one of the top ten in the world, come down and she tried out one of his violins that I have," claimed Jerald Humbert, who is now in his eighties and the grandson of William Marshall. "Well, she wanted to borrow it, take it back to Portland to play in a concert. I said no, I wasn't about to part with this heirloom treasure built by my granddad." Jerald, a resident of Salem, went on to relate an incident that he remembered from his Eastside childhood.

After one long session of tedious craftsmanship, William Humbert had finally completed a run of about a dozen violins. With a crinkled-up forehead he began to test play each one, tossing them aside one after another as the furrows of his brow deepened. Finally, in a fit of disgust, he crammed all of them into a gunny sack and commenced to jump up and down upon it, stomping his handiwork into smithereens.

In a final fit of rage and closure, Humbert dragged the gunny sack of broken violins outside the shop and set it afire. After having poured his heart into these creations, he'd destroyed them, erasing the hours of labor to begin anew. In an up-swelling of courage he'd rejected his own work that wasn't quite up to his ultimate standard, and looked ahead towards higher goals.

This brings to mind some lines from "If" by Rudyard Kipling:

> *"If you can watch the things you gave life to, broken,*
> *And stoop and build 'em up with worn out tools;*
> *And lose, and start again at your beginnings*
> *And never breathe a word of your loss."*

Well, Humbert may have breathed a few cuss words about his losses. We can only speculate.

Myrtle trees won't stop growing and the music doesn't stop playing. Fast forward to the 21st Century and we have a phoenix bird of myrtlewood rising from the Humbert ashes: the Breedlove Guitar Company of Bend, Oregon.

This company of luthiers has gradually embraced myrtlewood for its stringed instrument production. According to the owner of the company, Tom Bedell, "Myrtlewood has been a real breakthrough for us. Of all the tone woods that exist on earth, myrtlewood is one of the top two or three in terms of the sound it creates, right up there with rosewood and mahogany. Half of our USA Breedlove guitars made now feature it, and it remains in demand because of its sound qualities." The company claims to obtain its raw material from sustainable logging in the Coast Range mountains. Myrtlewood shops and their products may be in decline, but something always comes along to fill the gaps.

Wood Burns

Far more myrtlewood is burned than ever makes it to a product or art piece. Slash burns from logging attest to that and, after the standard practice of chipping any extra hardwoods, excessive amounts of myrtle trees are still left at logging sites. Although historically myrtlewood crofters have accessed the logs that they need, what they use is far less than what is actually cut in the everyday logging operations of Douglas fir.

When showing my art at a local event a gentleman approached me and described his work with a Coos County Road Department project. "We completely dredged the main stem Coquille River," he explained. Then, with a touch of remorse, he added, "Tons of woody debris, including lots of myrtle logs, root wads, and whole trees were piled up, stuff that had lain submerged for many decades or longer. Now that I see what you do with the myrtle, I wish we hadn't burned it all."

With a shell-shocked look, I imagined the treasure trove of valuable myrtlewood coming out of the Coquille watershed: fantastic burls, logs hundreds of years old with colorations and root formations beyond imagination, all preserved by being submerged. And all reduced to ashes.

On a much sadder note, two of my artist friends with whom I occasionally worked perished when their home studios and all of their current artworks burned to the ground in separate accidental fires. These tragic infernos took the life of Phil Clausen in 2014 and, two years later, that of Norman Gould. Phil was famous for his carved wood furnishings, much of it from myrtle that he sourced locally. Norman was an accomplished painter with an art degree who was involved in local art groups and exhibitions at the Coos Art Museum.

Forecasts from the Past

An early 1920s *Oregonian* newspaper quoted Mr. E.D. Duncan of a Coos Bay myrtlewood firm who states, "As the trees are very slow in their growth, I predict that in 20 years they will be used up and then myrtlewood novelties will be genuine antiques." Another news article from that time conceded that the supply of wood from the old trees has become more limited, and refers to former days when the supply was larger.

Still another 1920's newspaper made the claim that "the supply of available wood is becoming scarce, as old trees are being rapidly used up, and it will require untold years before the young trees reach a usable maturity."

In a report from 1916, the Chamber of Commerce of Marshfield (now the city of Coos Bay) undertook a study to see if rumors of impending shortages of myrtlewood were true.

In 1974, the Oregon Myrtlewood Association drafted a resolution based on the threat of a diminished resource with the plea for conservation of myrtle trees aimed at "the Forest Service, Bureau of Land Management, road building and right of way building agencies and all logging companies and that public awareness for the need of conservation of this natural resource be brought into focus." In summary, there have always been predictions of the demise of commercially viable myrtlewood, and all this time the industry has remained well sustained, right up until the time of this writing.

However, current supply compared with usages of the tree and, more importantly, access to mature trees, could be reaching a tipping point. "I would give it five years," says Ron Smith, a current major purveyor and supplier of quality myrtle logs and lumber. "It's not that the trees are disappearing...they're not. But the access to those trees is more limited by extra regulations imposed on the logging industry."

Is the crystal ball again amiss on the longevity of myrtle trees and the crofter's creations dependent upon them? The lack of access would slow down the availability, and if a dependable supply chain doesn't exist, neither will the businesses that depend on it for their livelihoods. At that point it will go back to Mr. Duncan's prediction made 100 years ago that existing items and art created from the wood will be "genuine antiques."

In E.D. Duncan's time, myrtles carpeted many river valleys with trees averaging 2' to 7' diameters. Imagine the mature-to-old growth myrtle forests choking off miles of bottomland in a seemingly endless supply of raw material for myrtlewood crofters who harvested trees as farmers cleared the land. But by the 1940s the disappearance of these prolific groves raised alarms among conservationists.

At that time, the preeminent forester Thornton T. Munger organized the Save the Myrtle Wood League, which then morphed into Save the Myrtle Woods, Inc., with the main objective to buy prime myrtle groves for public park protection and encouraging preservation elsewhere. Munger, a conservationist from Portland, was known to have gone head-to-head with logging companies to prevent clear-cutting of myrtle stands they owned in the Coos River watershed.

Although large, mature trees are less numerous, the future of the tree is relativity unthreatened, as it flourishes in its habitat. The myrtles are stubbornly prolific growers with shoots sprouting heavily from cut stumps, and fallen trees form nurse logs with equally aggressive sprouts. Seeds germinate continuously, especially in the rich loam of riverine areas.

Myrtlewood Futures

Ron Smith began cutting myrtlewood in 1977 and has provided many shops with lumber and products. He has also cut and installed myrtlewood flooring in a number of houses, including replacement work in homes that burned in recent Oregon wildfires. "My success with accessing the best myrtlewood logs and providing lumber for today's active shops is simple. I know and have worked with the many loggers and timber companies that are in the myrtlewood habitat every day, and I maintain a good relationship with them," he explained to me. "I use a pickup truck and large trailer to haul select logs a few at a time, usually to a small specialty mill whose owner I have known since high school. From there I distribute the lumber to shops and use it in my own operations like myrtlewood flooring. I have more orders for flooring then I can keep up with. I'm actually turning them down."

What logs Smith harvests and disperses for five of the remaining active shops and a handful of producers is adequate for now. Still, he laments that the lack of experienced workers, especially bowl turners to keep the industry progressing, is a problem. All evidence suggests that the demand for myrtlewood continues, but supplying finished products is in trouble. Since outlets have greatly diminished, small producers become discouraged and seek opportunities elsewhere. If skills and knowledge are not perpetuated and passed down, myrtlewood crofting is at risk of becoming a lost art. On the following pages I've listed 29 myrtlewood shops from the 1980s and the six active ones at this writing.

Hardscrabble operators salvaging myrtlewood on a limited scale continue to work the wood. Land owners of myrtle groves are set to harvest and produce products from their own backyard, and sell them out the front door as James Humbert did in Powers, Oregon for many years. Gerry Deadmond, a long-time crofter as well as a currently active myrtlewood sales rep, has provided a liaison between wholesale producers and retail shops statewide for decades.

David Groth, who creates and sells all his artwork from myrtlewood salvaged from the Northern California beaches, is among a handful of current artists with predict-able supplies. As long as seasonal floods wash material out of the mountains his resource will stay intact, and he will continue to produce his large, fantastical creations.

Today, none of the remaining myrtlewood shops cut their own logs, unlike in the recent past, with the excep-tion of the Myrtlewood Gallery of Reedsport, Oregon. It is likely that this family owned-and-operated gallery will perpetuate their lineage by working myrtlewood well into the future, the only shop continuing a myrtlewood family tradition similar to the old timers like the Oerdings. The pressure is on the Mast family dynasty, however, for they also have problems from a lack of suppliers, and are forced to produce an overload of products for their shelves. Yet all evidence suggests that this operation is continuing as the flagship myrtlewood center of the region.

In conclusion, the near-term threat to myrtlewood commerce is more a lack of skilled men and women crofters than a lack of resource. When product selection is limited, buyer interest diminishes, increasing the downward spiral of the myrtlewood crofter's legacy. This could balance out with the aforementioned musical instruments, the demand for fine furniture and flooring, a modest number of shops with their own products, and the reach of myrtlewood art creations. It remains to be seen how the vibrant, colorful past of this national treasure will be matched in the future.

Conservation of National Living Treasures

This national treasure tree exists as yet another tree in the forest. It could be said that it's just a tree, or its inner core is only wood, but it is something more, a spirit that entwines humans with the forest. It is the human endeavor that recognizes the inherent material found within, and transforms it into a valuable commodity of natural beauty. Conservation and wise use of this material can be accomplished, albeit only on a limited scale of production.

These treasures should be cut with reverence when their life span has been fulfilled. Their aged beauty and great character must be preserved in objects built of their wood to provide a record of their heritage and history.

—Master Woodcraftsman George Nakashima, in reference to all fine woods, from his book *The Soul of a Tree.*

MYRTLEWOOD HERITAGE: THE SHOPS

(all locations in Oregon)

Active Retail Shops, 2022

Rogue River Myrtlewood, Gold Beach
roguerivermyrtlewood.com

Wooden Nickel, Port Orford
oregonmyrtlewood.com

Myrtlewood Factory, North Bend
myrtlewood-hauserrvpark.com

Lakeshore Myrtlewood, Florence
lakeshoremyrtlewood.com

Myrtlewood Gallery, Reedsport
myrtlewoodgallery.com

Myrtlewood Factory Outlet, Garibaldi
myrtlewoodfactoryoutletgaribaldi.com

Active Retail Shops of the 1980s & 1990s

The Myrtle Burl, Coquille

Heritage Myrtlewood, Coos Bay

House of Myrtlewood, Coos Bay

G & B Myrtlewood, Coos Bay [Eastside]

Bayview Manufacturing's Myrtlewood Chalets (Portland, Ashland, Eugene, Newport, North Bend, Jacksonville)

Swede's Myrtlewood, Lincoln City

Stateline Myrtlewood, Brookings

Rogue River Myrtlewood, Gold Beach

Seagull Myrtlewood, Bandon

A & T Myrtlewood, Sixes

Lakeshore Myrtlewood, Florence

The Myrtle Tree, Yachats

Ernie's Myrtlewood, Grants Pass

Myrtlewood Products, Grants Pass

Vintage Myrtlewood, Ashland

Horizon Myrtlewood, Langlois

Myrtlewood Specialty Products, Roseburg

Pacific Myrtlewood, Laurel Grove

Candlestick Factory, Laurel Grove

Zumwalts Myrtlewood, Laurel Grove

The Table Factory, Tillamook

Myrtlewood Factory Outlet, Garibaldi

Myrtlewood Mystique Gallery, Philomath

Who's First?

In advertising and competition between businesses there is a tendency to showcase and broadcast who's the biggest and who's been around the longest. This sets a credibility factor to attract business, and these anthems played out among myrtlewood businesses as well. Bayview Manufacturing Company swept the modern field for size and number of outlets (although there were some large factory operations in the 1920s).

So, who's first? According to the previous accounts, the Oerdings were the first producers and distributers of products, beginning in 1907. But wait a minute, if it comes down to who established the first business specializing in myrtlewood, no matter how humble, the first myrtlewood shop? That would have to be—and the Who's First Award goes to—MR.FISH!! Although it was likely a one-man shop and he may have bartered as much as he sold, as far as we know, Mr. Fish owned the first actual original myrtlewood shop, located in the early settlement of Coquille, Oregon, and an inspiration for the Oerding dynasty that followed.

Other information available on myrtlewood:

"Myrtlewood, Oregon's Tropical Hardwood," a comprehensive DVD on myrtlewood produced in 2006 by Mike Merica, Rogue River Myrtlewood, Gold Beach, Oregon.

"Myrtlewood Country" brochure, produced by the Oregon Myrtlewood Association and Oregon State Parks and Recreation Department, 1994; fifth release, 2012.

THE GREATEST MYRTLEWOOD SHOW ON EARTH! INTERVIEW

While researching recent history of myrtle land, I managed an interview with Mike Erbele, a North Bend, Oregon business owner and former city council member of that city, who had a key role in B. Roger Clark's initial construction and operation of the world's largest myrtlewood factory. In the following interview Mike reflects on those years.

Terry: Mike, How did you know B. Roger Clark?

Mike: We met at an equipment show and sale in Portland. I worked in a furniture factory there that went out of business, and we were selling equipment. Roger bought some spray booths, but all he wanted was the motors that went with them, so I helped him dismantle them. He wanted me to go to work for him in the town of North Bend, to manage his myrtlewood factory. I'd never heard of the place, but he kept egging me on, encouraging me to give it a try. Finally, I gave in, went down there to look it over. I never left.

Terry: You eventually bought the same building for your own business. How did that happen?

Mike: I worked for Roger on the factory floor for three years, starting in 1973. Then he built the new mega factory north of town in 1974. It was up and running by 1975. I helped him move equipment to the new site, even did all the electric work in the new buildings. It was called Bayview Manufacturing Company. Well, that left his original myrtlewood shop empty. I started my own cabinet business and bought the building by 1978.

Terry: That would be Lamco, right?

Mike: Yes, Lamco custom cabinets, still in operation at the same location.

Terry: What do you know about your building? How long was it a myrtlewood shop?

Mike: It was built in 1937 by Roger Duncan for a myrtlewood shop and factory. He managed to salvage high quality beams from the construction of the new Coos Bay jetty and used them in this building. They were top-grade timbers because the jetty was built to Army Corps of Engineers specs. Then John Reiher owned and operated it.

Terry: As a myrtlewood shop?

Mike: Yes, it continued as such right up until Roger Clark left. Roger bought it in 1970 and opened his Myrtlewood Chalet gift shop with a factory making the products in the back.

Terry: Why did he make the move to a new factory?

Mike: His business strategy was to go wholesale based on maximizing production. He already had five retail store outlets in Portland, Ashland, Jacksonville, one in Pony Village Mall here in town, and the Myrtlewood Chalet in this building with the factory. Actually, they were all called Myrtlewood Chalet. He needed to keep them supplied and expand wholesale accounts, which he did worldwide.

Terry: He eventually increased these outlets to include Eugene and Newport, Oregon, right?

Mike: Yes, he juggled around his many Chalet store outlets. Those came later on.

Terry: Bayview Manufacturing no longer exists. What happened?

Mike: The jump he made from retail to wholesale killed the business... too much overhead with the large factory.

Also, he lost the tour bus stops that he'd established in the town shop. His chief competitor, the House of Myrtlewood, picked up the tour bus visits.

Terry: Roger kept the factory fully operating until he sold it and retired?

Mike: Yes, but the new owners weren't experienced enough with myrtlewood and machining of the wood. It went downhill from then on.

Terry: Even the early factories of the 1920s were successful selling in places like New York. Why wasn't Bayview?

Mike: It takes much more to float large-scale manufacturing today, and there just isn't the name that makes myrtlewood special outside of Oregon. If you have, say, a Macy's in New York with a shelf lined with teak, monkey pod, and myrtlewood items, the myrtle gets lost in the mix.

Terry: When I came on board in 1979, tourism seemed to be booming on the Oregon Coast, and so were the sales of myrtlewood and its production.

Mike: No, it was never the same after the gas crisis.

Terry: Are you referring to the gas shortages of 1973 and 1979?

Mike: Yes, the tourism on our coast was never the same again. There was much more activity before those slowdowns, and it never recovered to the same level as before. Also, people started flying more, and that never stopped.

Terry: Did you remain friends with Roger after your business splits?

Mike: Oh yes, we went to high-school football games together, and I attended his daughter's wedding. I was the shortest person there; they were all tall like Roger!

IN MEMORIAM

There were many, many workers of myrtlewood from the early 20th century through the present. Those acknowledged below were active from the 1970s on, and most were known personally by the author. Of those not mentioned, the author apologizes, as they are of no less importance for it.

Chuck & Georgianne Alcock

Don Barber

Tricia (Streeter) Benetti

B. Roger Clark

Lee Dean

Ron Foster

Robert Harbison

James Humbert

John Reiher

George Stovall

Bob Tuck

John & Myrna Austin

Lloyd Bechtel

Ed Benshoof

Phil Clausen

De Long

Abe Hanks

Edsil Hodge

Robert Oerding

Dan Scoville

Les Streeter

Aggie Wasteny

FREEING
THE
BIRDS

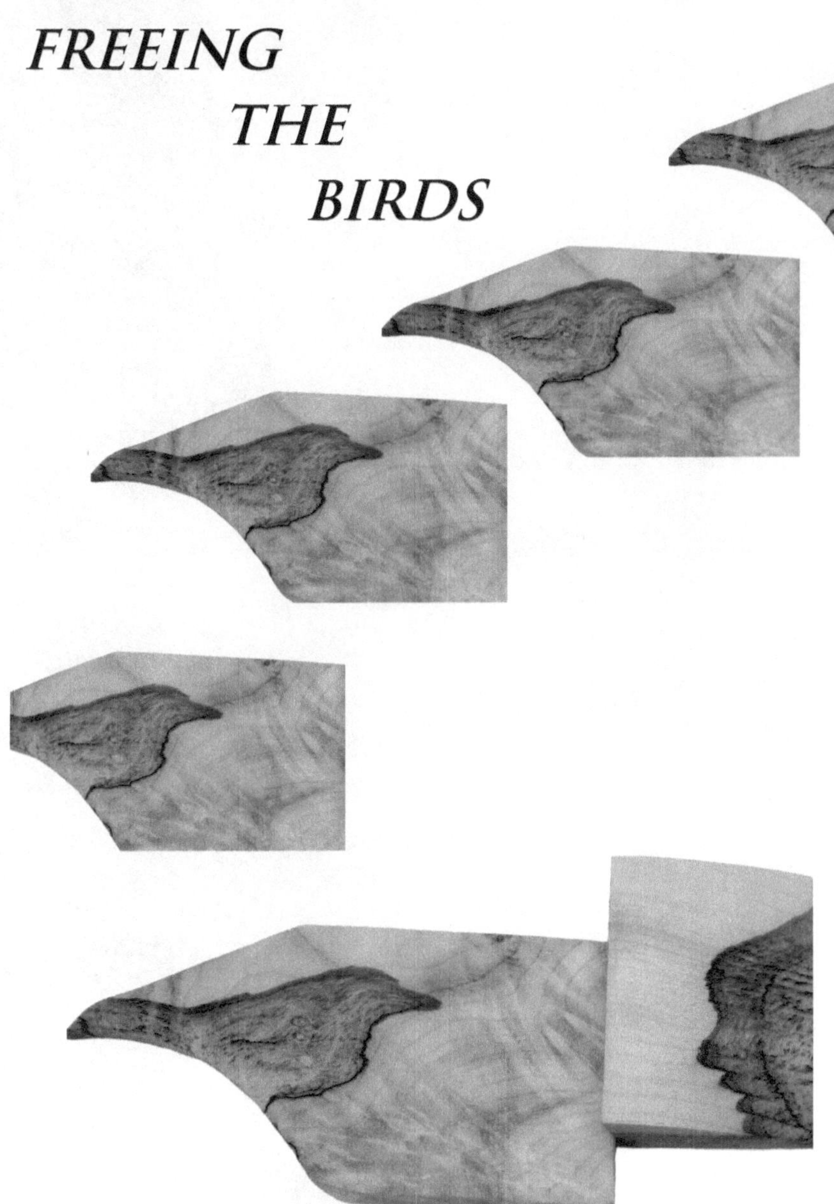

The mind can work on sensory stimulation, such as a complex cloud formation, to perceive something recognizable. I have applied this process to years of studying complex grain patterns in myrtlewood, and have managed to save out many outstanding likenesses to human, animal, and bird figures. Birds freed from the wood grain resulted in the images on these pages, including drawings (next page) with natural images superimposed into the sketches.

Treebird Camo

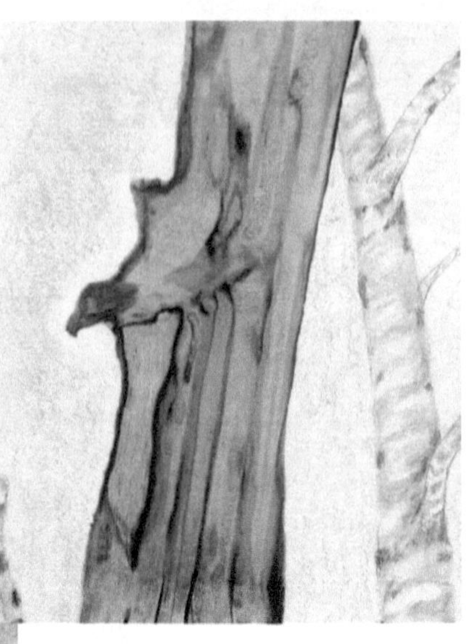

Vulture Alights, Awaits

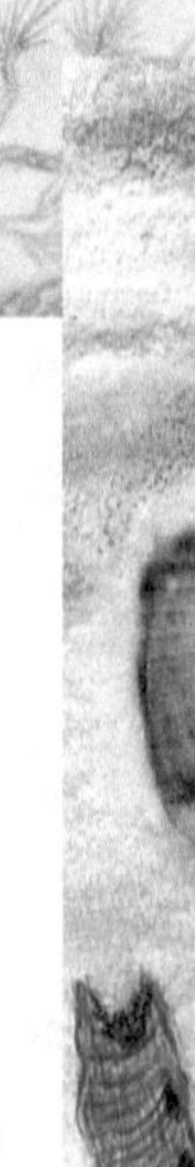

Clustering

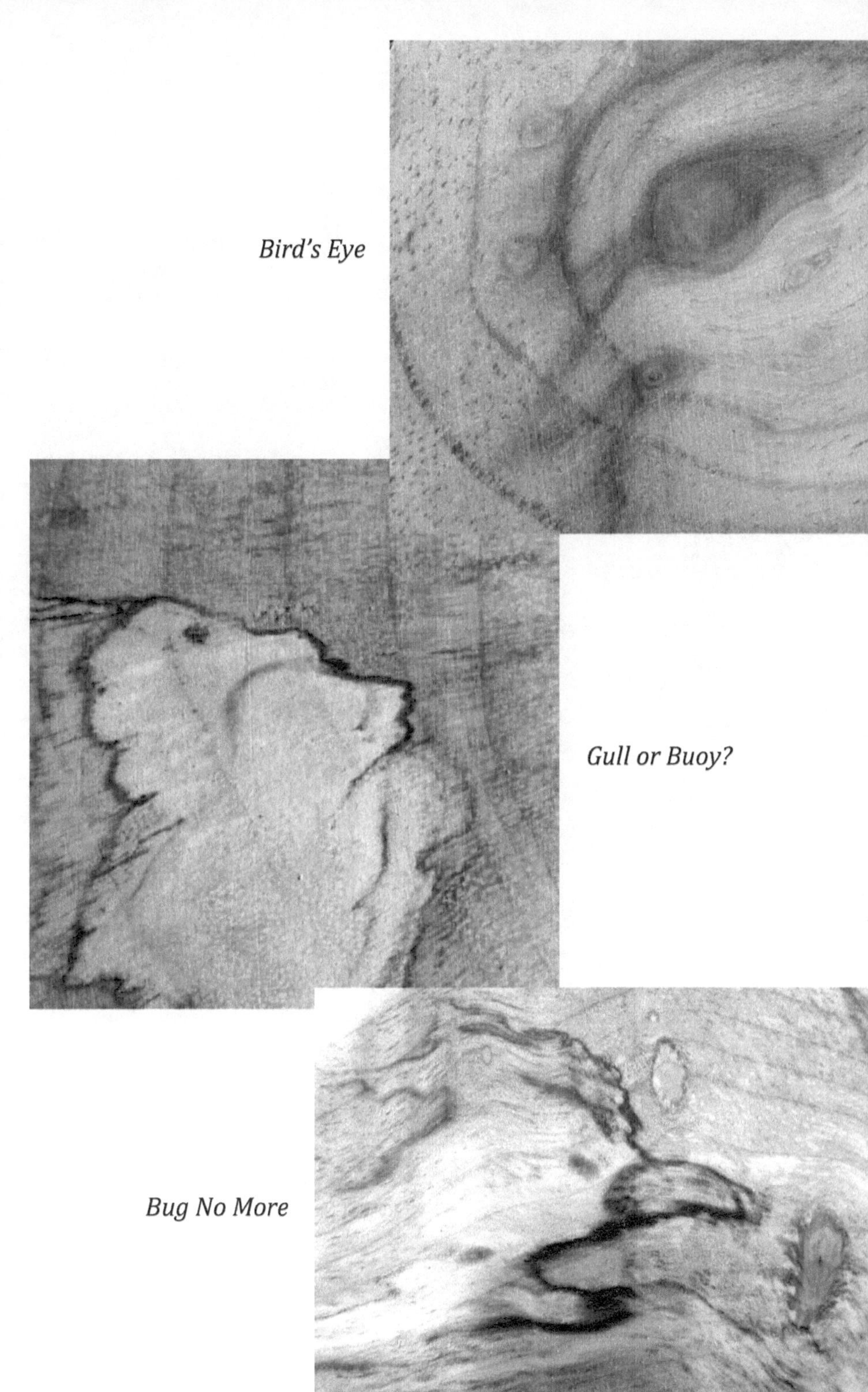

Bird's Eye

Gull or Buoy?

Bug No More

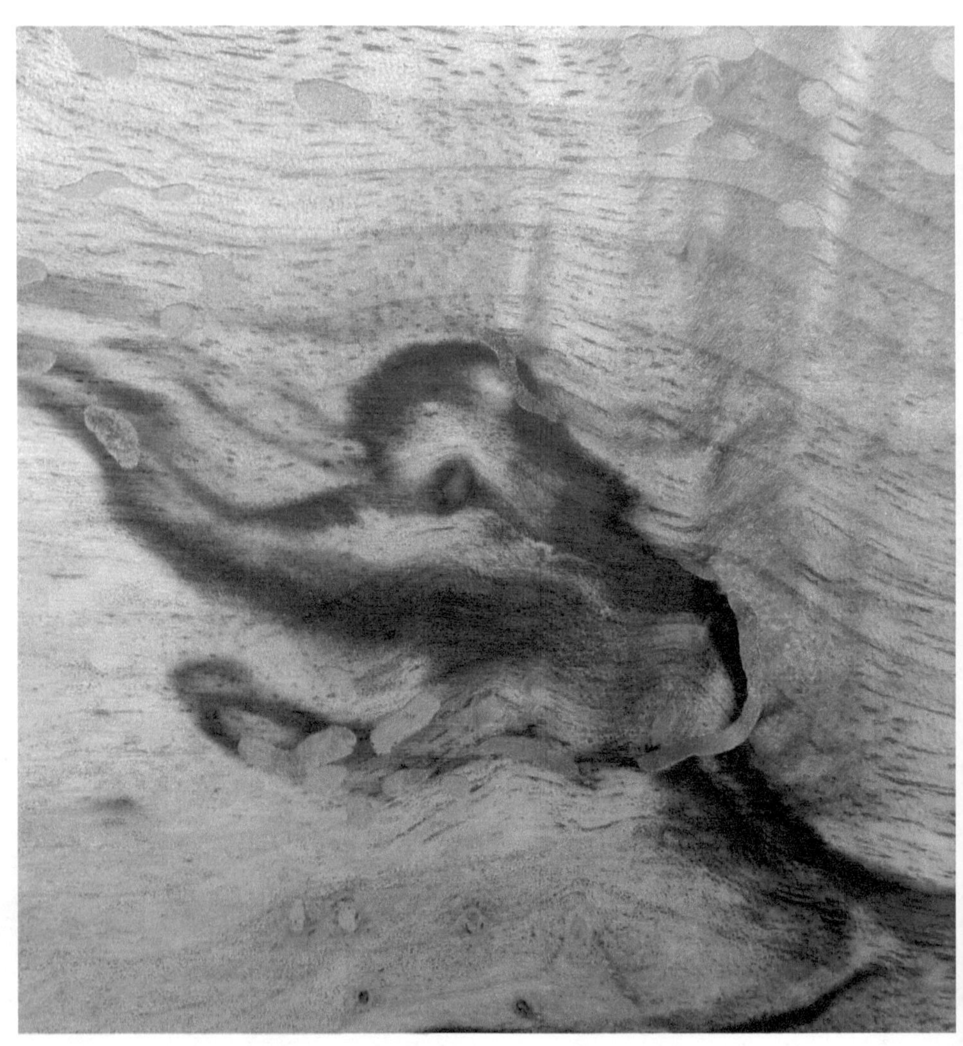

Tell me, what do you see?

Comment at www.terrywoodall.wordpress.com

ABOUT THE AUTHOR

Terry Woodall is an accomplished writer on nature and nature art whose articles have appeared in *Artists for Conservation* online, *Wildlife Art Journal* webzine, the former *Wildlife Art Magazine*, the *Society of Animal Artists* newsletter, and his own art and travels blogs, one of which was also published by a Stanford University blog site. He is a member of the Society of Animal Artists and the Artists for Conservation Foundation.

Woodall was awarded an Artists for Conservation Flag Expedition Fellowship, which gave him the opportunity for an artistic field study to Lake Baikal, Russia. From the experiences of this flag expedition, Woodall wrote and illustrated a comprehensive leather-bound journal covering his Siberian adventure for the benefit of the AFC Foundation. His one-person art show at The Nature Museum, Irkutsk, Russia exhibited many of his myrtlewood marine art creations, specifically seal renditions.

Woodall shares his knowledge and appreciation for nature and wildlife in lectures sponsored by the Oregon State Parks Department. Of note are his lectures on the freshwater Baikal Seals and sculpture demonstrations at the Art of Conservation exhibitions in Vancouver, B.C., Canada, and the AFC art exhibition at the Hiram Blauvelt Art Museum, Oradell, New Jersey.

He has also exhibited at the Mall Galleries, London, where he was a finalist for the David Shepherd Wildlife Foundation's tenth annual Wildlife Artist of the Year Award, and exhibited numerous times with the Society of Animal

Artists, the Artists for Conservation, and the Coos Art Museum's Maritime Art Exhibits. His work was selected for the "Endangered Species, Flora and Fauna in Peril" art exhibition and national tour sponsored by the Wildling Museum, Solvang, California, which included a showing at the Department of the Interior Museum, Washington, D.C.

Primarily, Terry Woodall is an internationally exhibited artist who creates spectacular wildlife sculpture in both wood and bronze. His flawless technical abilities and deep-seated connection to his subjects come alive in every unique work of art. His imaginative use of form and flawless use of negative and positive space and his attention to detail culminate in his extraordinary signature style.

—Renee Phillips, founder and director,
Manhattan Arts International, New York, New York

View the author's artwork at www.terrywoodall.com and watch for his full-color book of art and stories, **Myrtlewood Memoirs: the Wildlife Art**, coming soon. For more writings by the author visit www.terrywoodall.wordpress.com

Back cover: Photo of the author. Lower photo: Free-form myrtlewood sculpture of the rare sokoke scops owl. An 8" x 8" photographic tile of this piece is part of the Artists for Conservation's 100' Silent Skies Mural, a collective of the world's 678 endangered birds, each one depicted by artists on separate tiles; at www.artistsforconservation.org/silent-skies.